LORILEE LUCAS

The Ultimate Self-Care Handbook

1000+ Hassle-Free Ideas to Escape Burnout, Reduce Stress and Reclaim Your Life

For permission requests, wholesale orders or speaking engagements, contact Everwell Publishing at everwellpublishing@gmail.com

First edition

This book was professionally typeset on Reedsy.
Find out more at reedsy.com

To the Universe, whose boundless gifts have taught me the art of resilience.
To myself, for the courage to embrace each challenge with a spirit of play.
And to the beautiful souls who enrich my life, mirroring back the magic of every moment.

Contents

1 INTRODUCTION TO SELF-CARE   1
2 NERVOUS SYSTEM REGULATION   23
3 PHYSICAL SELF-CARE   50
4 MENTAL SELF-CARE   63
5 EMOTIONAL SELF-CARE   75
6 SOCIAL SELF-CARE   92
7 PROFESSIONAL SELF-CARE   104
8 FINANCIAL SELF-CARE   117
9 INTELLECTUAL SELF-CARE   127
10 SPIRITUAL SELF-CARE   135
11 RECREATIONAL SELF-CARE   145
12 ENVIRONMENTAL SELF-CARE   152
13 THE ROAD TO CHANGE   165
14 A NOTE OF GRATITUDE   168
15 RESOURCES   171
16 About the Author   178

1

INTRODUCTION TO SELF-CARE

Our lives are built around core commitments—family, work, school, and community. While these bring great joy and fulfillment, there is also a strong likelihood that amidst the ceaseless clamor, we have felt a great deal of stress, overwhelm, and, on occasion, complete burnout. Life is full of constant change, and it is within this ebb and flow that we are called to embark on the quiet revolution of self-care. At its simplest, self-care is the practice of protecting and enhancing our well-being. It involves prioritizing our needs and engaging in activities that support our body, uplift our spirit, calm our mind, and regulate our emotions and nervous system. It is the art of nurturing one's soul.

Self-care is deeply personal and subjective. What feels nurturing and supportive to you may feel uncomfortable or restrictive to another. For instance, a close friend of mine finds her greatest joy tending to her garden or immersing herself in a good book to start her day, while another swears by long runs with her running group to clear her mind and stay connected with her community. I have discovered that calming music and the moving meditation of a yoga class help me to get clarity and focus for my day. These varied approaches emphasize that self-care is not one-size-fits-all; it is about finding what truly works for you and leaning into those practices without comparison to others or judgment. Some people find solace in quiet solitude or meditation, while others may thrive in social environments or through active pursuits like hiking or dancing. These differences highlight the importance of tuning into your preferences and needs rather than following a one-size-fits-all approach. By honoring what genuinely resonates with you, self-care becomes a practice of self-discovery and authenticity. Know that this is okay and perfectly natural. This gets to the heart of the self-care voyage: deepening self-awareness, listening to the needs and concerns that arise within you, and drawing from resources to create a customized approach that works for you. By taking the self-assessment quiz included, you can quickly identify areas of your current self-care routine that you excel at and those that could use more support. The quiz results can guide your approach to using this book. An extensive array of self-care strategies is organized by category, allowing you to quickly hone in on ideas and action items to help balance your routine.

Given the ever-changing nature of life, it's only natural that your self-care needs will evolve as well. You might notice this shift through subtle signs, like feeling more irritable or drained by activities that once energized you or through major life changes, such as a new job, a move, or a significant relationship shift. These moments are opportunities to reassess and adapt. For instance, you might find that practices like journaling or deep breathing, which once sufficed, now need to be complemented with additional tools such as regular exercise or therapy. Being attuned to these changes ensures that your self-care regimen remains aligned with your current needs, helping you navigate life's fluctuations with greater ease. Daily fluctuations, monthly shifts, and yearly transformations all play a role in shaping your unique self-care regimen. Embrace these changes—they are a normal part of living a full life. It is best thought of as an ever-changing landscape instead of a goalpost to be achieved and maintained. Self-care extends far beyond mere indulgence or temporary escapes. It embodies a profound commitment to stewarding your energy and time effectively. This dedication to self-care is not just about maintaining wellness; it's about honoring and respecting the body that houses your spirit throughout your journey on earth. By prioritizing self-care, you consciously nurture and protect your well-being, ensuring you can thrive and adapt regardless of life's unpredictable waves.

My connection to self-care became deeply personal after a life-altering near-death experience in 2007. This event not only reshaped my perspective on life but also crystallized my philosophy on self-care. In those vulnerable moments, overwhelmed by a profound sense of fragility and uncertainty, it forced me to reevaluate how I approached life. The sense of being a guardian and caretaker for the gift of my body, mind, and spirit became more obvious and highlighted how my choices had unintentionally led to this extremely close call. From this physically weakened and emotionally raw place, a deep determination was ignited within me to rebuild my body and spirit. This required a massive restructuring of my belief system as well as radical honesty with myself around my concept of self-worth and self-love. I realized that prioritizing self-care was not a luxury but a necessity—a sacred act of survival and renewal. During this time, I had no other choice. I had to turn inward to protect the flicker of life that remained, focusing on rebuilding my body and restoring my zest for life. In many ways, this experience prepared me for what was to come. My commitment to self-care deepened in 2020 following a cascade of losses. I lost my home in a California wildfire, my career and financial stability to the COVID-19 industry collapse, and I experienced the heart-breaking dissolution of my long-term marriage shortly after. During this period, I was also diagnosed with systemic mold illness, which affected multiple organ systems and placed additional strain on my physical, mental, emotional, and financial resources.

With so many aspects of life simultaneously challenged all at once, conducting personal triage and prioritizing my needs became a necessity. The self-assessment test within this book was borne of this personal triage system I developed. Instead of compiling to-do lists, which would have filled an overwhelming number of notebooks, making it difficult to prioritize, I got really good at scanning how I felt at any given moment and asking myself what I needed that day or week to keep my nervous system regulated and grounded by what really matters.

I learned the importance of setting clear boundaries and practicing assertive communication as essential tools in self-care. During this time, I was often exhausted—overwhelmed with the enormity of rebuilding our lives from the ground up with the limited energy I had due to the taxing health issues mold illness brings. Setting boundaries with myself and others became utterly critical. Forcing myself to carve out an hour every day to get outside and hike with my family created space within the chaos to connect with my husband, play with the dogs, clear my head, and reconnect with nature in a positive way to de-emphasize the fear and negativity I had experienced with the wildfire. I also became incredibly selective in the social engagements I accepted. The experiences I engaged in had to fill my "energy tank" because I simply had nothing left to give.

True friends committed to reciprocity experienced my newfound assertive communication skills as a friendly way to explain my needs with kindness and clarity. Those who were used to quick and easy access to my support, advice, or time but did not have this type of mindset experienced assertive communication as rejection or annoyance. It highlighted the transactional nature of those relationships and helped me to see more clearly that they were not equal exchanges to begin with and made it easier to let them go.

The honest acknowledgment of where I was at and what I was both capable and willing to engage in set the stage to reorganize my new life around the principle of protecting my peace. Boundaries are not walls to shut others out or to attempt to control them. They are bridges to healthier relationships—both with others and ourselves. Assertive communication skills reinforce those boundaries to ensure that our needs are met while also respecting the needs of those around us. This balance creates a foundation for mutual understanding, growth, and harmony.

Remember, self-care isn't just another task on your to-do list. Instead, consider it a foundational practice supporting every aspect of your life. While this book offers many suggestions and ideas—presented in a checklist format—you're not expected to adopt every single one. Approaching it this way would be more overwhelming than helpful. Pace yourself.

Tune into your emotions and let them steer you through your self-care journey.

We will explore the barriers that hinder our capacity for self-care and illuminate pathways to fulfillment. These barriers may include societal pressures to prioritize productivity over well-being, the challenges of saying no, feelings of guilt or inadequacy, and the lack of practical tools to implement lasting changes. By addressing these obstacles head-on, you will be empowered to make meaningful shifts in your approach to self-care. Drawing on ancient wisdom and insights from psychology, philosophy, and cutting-edge research, this book offers a wealth of ideas to spark your creativity in designing a personalized self-care plan. In particular, we delve into the realms of biohacking, neuroplasticity, and quantum physics to explore how our choices shape our reality. Self-care is a decisive step toward creating the life of your dreams by building the energy reserves needed to achieve them.

I invite you to approach this journey with an open heart and a curious mind. May this book serve as a compass to guide you toward greater self-awareness, compassion, and love—time and time again. As you explore the concepts and practices within these pages, remember that self-care is a journey, not a destination. There will be moments of triumph and times when you feel like you're starting over, but each step forward strengthens your foundation. With each practice you embrace, you are choosing to nurture your mind, body, and soul. By doing so, you not only transform your own life but also inspire those around you to do the same. Together, we can create a ripple effect of healing and empowerment, proving that even the smallest acts of self-care can lead to profound change. By refining your ability to replenish and rejuvenate, you not only enhance your own life but also become a beacon of healing and light for others.

SELF-CARE ASSESSMENT/QUIZ

The following Self-Care Assessment provides a framework to assess your current strengths and areas for improvement in various self-care categories. This list is not exhaustive, but it offers valuable insight into your present habits. Please be as honest as possible with yourself. Focus on your current reality rather than your past habits or future goals. Pay attention to any thoughts or feelings that arise while scoring yourself, as they may highlight key areas for personal growth.

Rate each category based on how well you believe you are doing right now:

4 = I excel at this!
This is part of my consistent, regular routine. It is a habit.

3 = I do this well.
I do this frequently but not consistently. It isn't a habit.

2 = I do this ok.
This is something I do occasionally.

1 = I rarely or never do this.

Once you've completed the assessment, tally your points for each area, then organize the list by highest to lowest score.

PHYSICAL SELF-CARE

☐ I eat regular, balanced meals (breakfast, lunch, dinner).

☐ I prioritize healthy, whole foods and limit junk food and sweets.

☐ I moderate alcohol consumption and avoid smoking or vaping.

☐ I avoid illicit substances and responsibly use prescribed medications.

☐ I engage in at least 30 minutes of physical activity daily.

☐ I schedule regular doctor and dental checkups.

☐ I take time off work when sick to focus on recovery.

☐ I prioritize sexual wellness with myself and/or my partner(s).

☐ I maintain a consistent bedtime and optimize my sleep environment.

☐ I limit screen time (phone, computer, TV, tablet) to an hour before bed.

☐ I brush and floss my teeth daily.

☐ I bathe or shower regularly.

☐ I maintain personal hygiene (hair care, deodorant, clean clothes)

☐ I feel confident and comfortable in my body.

☐ I notice body tension and use strategies to release it effectively.

☐ **Total Points (Physical)**

MENTAL SELF-CARE

☐ I am aware of my inner thoughts, beliefs, and emotions.

☐ I journal to process, reflect, and integrate my experiences.

☐ I seek support from friends or family when struggling.

☐ I consult professionals (therapist, coach, counselor) when needed.

☐ I understand my attachment style and work to improve relationships.

☐ I process past traumas rather than powering through unresolved issues.

☐ I address dissatisfaction or imbalance in my life proactively.

☐ I practice mindfulness, meditation, or restorative exercises like yoga.

☐ I say no to commitments that overwhelm my capacity.

☐ I avoid gossiping or reliving past traumas in a triggering way.

☐ I celebrate my successes and progress.

☐ I show self-compassion in areas where I'm still growing.

☐ I forgive myself when I fall short of my expectations.

☐ I apologize and make amends when I've caused harm.

☐ I prioritize creating a safe, calm environment for myself.

☐ **Total Points (Environmental)**

EMOTIONAL SELF-CARE

☐ I laugh deeply and smile often.

☐ I recognize and name my emotions.

☐ I communicate my feelings to others.

☐ I use healthy coping strategies instead of numbing behaviors.

☐ I limit exposure to negative influences (e.g., toxic media or people).

☐ I celebrate my achievements.

☐ I nurture a supportive social network.

☐ I spend quality time with people and pets that bring me joy.

☐ I develop emotional intelligence by managing triggers and responses.

☐ I move my body regularly to boost my mood.

☐ I use breathing exercises or visualization to pause before reacting.

☐ I feel aligned with my life's purpose.

☐ I maintain balanced, reciprocal relationships.

☐ I find growth and meaning even in challenging experiences.

☐ I set boundaries to protect my time and emotional energy.

☐ **Total Points (Emotional)**

SOCIAL SELF-CARE

☐ I prioritize social connections that fulfill my needs.

☐ I show up authentically in my relationships.

☐ I value quality over quantity in building meaningful connections.

☐ I listen actively and participate in reciprocal conversations.

☐ I keep my commitments to myself and others.

☐ I embrace opportunities to make new friends when space allows.

☐ I ask for and offer help when needed.

☐ I express gratitude through thank-you notes or verbal acknowledgments.

☐ I share openly with trusted individuals.

☐ I respond to messages promptly.

☐ I honor others' vulnerability and avoid gossiping.

☐ I respect boundaries and say no when necessary.

☐ I give and receive compliments and gratitude with ease.

☐ I remain curious and seek clarity in relationships when needed.

☐ I practice forgiveness to repair and strengthen connections.

☐ **Total Points (Social)**

PROFESSIONAL SELF-CARE

☐ I maintain a healthy work-life balance to prevent burnout.

☐ I manage my time effectively to stay focused at work.

☐ I take regular breaks for rest, movement, and hydration.

☐ I build a supportive network of colleagues.

☐ I have mentors who guide my career growth.

☐ I prepare healthy snacks and meals to maintain energy.

☐ I share my ideas and opinions in meetings.

☐ I pursue professional development opportunities.

☐ I advocate for myself in workload, promotions, and work-life balance.

☐ I view failures as opportunities for growth.

☐ I use assertive communication to address conflicts.

☐ I delegate tasks to reduce stress and empower others.

☐ I create an ergonomic and comfortable workspace.

☐ I stay updated on technology and marketable skills.

☐ I seek feedback and set growth goals.

☐ **Total Points (Professional)**

FINANCIAL SELF-CARE

- ☐ I stick to a budget that tracks income and expenses.
- ☐ I maintain an emergency fund for unexpected costs.
- ☐ I set and actively work toward financial goals.
- ☐ I manage debt responsibly or prioritize paying it off.
- ☐ I contribute to a retirement plan.
- ☐ I diversify investments for safety and growth.
- ☐ I educate myself on personal finance topics.
- ☐ I believe in abundance and financial stability.
- ☐ I live within my means and avoid impulsive spending.
- ☐ I have a financial plan for both short- and long-term goals.
- ☐ I've established an estate plan with necessary documents.
- ☐ I track my net worth and align it with my goals.
- ☐ I ensure housing costs stay below 30% of my income.
- ☐ I pay bills on time and dispute errors promptly.
- ☐ I cross-check statements regularly and dispute erroneous charges.

☐ **Total Points (Financial)**

INTELLECTUAL SELF-CARE

☐ I read regularly to expand my knowledge.

☐ I engage with educational content like podcasts and documentaries.

☐ I protect my brain health by avoiding harmful substances.

☐ I have stimulating conversations.

☐ I enjoy activities that challenge my cognitive skills (e.g., puzzles).

☐ I engage in sensory activities like cooking or crafting.

☐ I stimulate memory and language through learning and cultural immersion.

☐ I practice visualization and creativity through art or guided imagery.

☐ I support motor skills with yoga, dance, or fine motor activities.

☐ I prioritize brain health with exercise, nutrition, and rest.

☐ I wear protective gear like helmets when needed.

☐ I develop emotional intelligence and practice empathy.

☐ I try new experiences and hobbies regularly.

☐ I explore cultural events and enrich my perspective.

☐ I support brain health with supplements and green tea.

☐ **Total Points (Intellectual)**

SPIRITUAL SELF-CARE

☐ I reflect regularly on my values and purpose.

☐ My beliefs help me stay aligned with my life's mission.

☐ I connect with a spiritual community.

☐ I spend time in nature to recharge and find peace.

☐ I look for positivity in difficult situations.

☐ I value non-material aspects of life.

☐ I let my values guide my decisions.

☐ I find inspiration in acts of goodness.

☐ I give back through service and kindness.

☐ I engage in prayer, meditation, or devotional practices.

☐ I contribute to causes I believe in.

☐ I connect with a higher power or universal order.

☐ I honor rituals that support my spirituality.

☐ I practice daily gratitude.

☐ I aim to embody kindness and compassion.

☐ **Total Points (Spiritual)**

RECREATIONAL SELF-CARE

☐ I schedule time for play and enjoyment.

☐ I try new activities and explore new hobbies.

☐ I embrace humor and don't take myself too seriously.

☐ I stay present during downtime without multitasking.

☐ I spend time outdoors engaging in recreational activities.

☐ I express creativity through various projects or crafts.

☐ I balance work and play, enjoying life's ebb and flow.

☐ I cherish hobbies that bring me joy.

☐ I laugh often and appreciate humor.

☐ I pair mundane tasks with fun to make them enjoyable.

☐ I approach life with childlike curiosity and wonder.

☐ I dress up and celebrate occasions playfully.

☐ I create playlists and enjoy music that lifts my mood.

☐ I maintain a bucket list of exciting experiences.

☐ I explore nature and embrace cultural adventures.

☐ **Total Points (Recreational)**

ENVIRONMENTAL SELF-CARE

☐ I keep my car clean and clutter-free.

☐ I make my bed daily.

☐ I declutter and avoid hoarding unnecessary items.

☐ I keep my home and workspace at a comfortable temperature.

☐ I organize and maintain a tidy home/office.

☐ I regularly clear out expired or unwanted items, like food.

☐ I minimize noise pollution for a peaceful environment.

☐ I follow a weekly cleaning routine.

☐ I maintain a tidy garage or storage space.

☐ I keep plants that purify the air in my home.

☐ I maximize natural light and use appropriate lighting for activities.

☐ I create a pleasant ambiance with scents or a neutral environment for sensitivities.

☐ I wash linens and towels weekly.

☐ I check for and address mold or mildew promptly.

☐ I open windows for fresh air when possible.

☐ **Total Points (Environmental)**

HOW TO USE THESE RESULTS

Now that you've completed the assessment and tallied your points for each category, organize your scores from highest to lowest using the template below:

_____ points, _____ (category of self-care)
_____ points, _____ (category of self-care)
_____ points, _____ (category of self-care)
_____ points, _____ (category of self-care)
_____ points, _____ (category of self-care)
_____ points, _____ (category of self-care)
_____ points, _____ (category of self-care)
_____ points, _____ (category of self-care)
_____ points, _____ (category of self-care)
_____ points, _____ (category of self-care)

SCORING GUIDE

40-60 points: Strong Self-Care Habits
20-40 points: Moderate Self-Care Engagement
0-20 points: Needs Attention

ANALYZING YOUR RESULTS

- How many categories of 10 self-care are in the 40-60 range?
- How many categories of 10 self-care are in the 20-40 range?
- How many categories of 10 self-care are in the 0-20 range?
- What do you notice about the spread of your points?
- Do you have a similar number of categories in each scoring range, or is the bulk of your rankings bucketed into one or two rankings?

SELF-REFLECTION AND NEXT STEPS

Celebrate Your Wins

Take time to acknowledge and appreciate the areas where you scored strongly. Recognizing your successes builds confidence, reinforces self-worth, and serves as a reminder of the healthy routines you've already established.

Identify Quick Wins

Look for small, manageable adjustments that could boost your scores in the Average range. Consistency, frequency, or minor tweaks in your routine can often lead to noticeable improvements.

Focus on Growth Opportunities

Prioritize intentional changes for categories in the Needs Work range. Explore the book sections tied to those areas for practical strategies and ideas to integrate into your life.

STRATEGIES BY SCORING RANGE

40–60 Points: "Strong" Categories

- Are any of your strong categories surprising? I'd like you to reflect on how your actions align with your self-perception.
- Do these routines feel uninspired or monotonous? If so, consider exploring fresh ideas to reinvigorate your approach.
- Can you integrate new strategies into existing habits ("bundling") to enhance your overall self-care?
- Consider reflecting on how these strengths can serve as a foundation for growth in other areas.

20–40 Points: "Average" Categories

- Find opportunities for small shifts in frequency/consistency to move categories into the Strong range.
- Reflect on past habits. Are there areas you previously excelled in but have since deprioritized? Visualize how it felt to thrive in those areas and use this as motivation.
- Assess potential barriers. Do you need additional resources, support, or professional guidance to improve?
- Start with small, achievable steps. Use the tools and strategies in this book to inspire action and enhance your routines.

0–20 Points: "Needs Work" Categories

- Low scores may indicate chronic stress, overwhelm, or burnout. If this resonates, your first priority should be addressing your nervous system regulation.
- Begin with the book's first chapter on Nervous System Regulation. Focus on calming and settling your body before tackling other self-care strategies.
- Allow yourself grace. Progress takes time, and prioritizing foundational well-being will enable you to revisit the assessment with greater capacity and energy.

MOVING FORWARD WITH INTENTION

Your self-care journey is a dynamic, evolving process. Celebrate the steps you've already taken, explore areas for improvement, and approach growth with curiosity and compassion. By refining your habits and routines, you'll create a more balanced, fulfilling life and strengthen your resilience to navigate life's challenges.

Remember, self-care is not about perfection—it's about progress. With every step, you're investing in your well-being and building a foundation for a healthier, more vibrant you.

2

NERVOUS SYSTEM REGULATION

*"Sometimes the most important thing in a whole day is
the rest we take between two deep breaths." - Etty
Hillesum*

The nervous system is a complex network of nerves and cells that controls our body's response to the world around us. It plays a fundamental role in the intricate dance of self-care, yet it is often overlooked. To fully understand the importance of our nervous systems within the framework of self-care, we need to briefly outline the components of this important part of our bodies.

The nervous system is a complex network of nerves, cells, and tissues that coordinates and regulates the body's activities and responses to the environment. It is divided into two main parts: the central nervous system (CNS) and the peripheral nervous system (PNS).

Central Nervous System (CNS): The CNS consists of

the brain and spinal cord. It serves as the command center of the body, receiving and processing sensory information from the environment, initiating appropriate responses, and coordinating the activities of various organ systems. The brain is responsible for higher cognitive functions such as thinking, memory, and emotions, while the spinal cord acts as a relay between the brain and the rest of the body, transmitting signals to and from the brain.

Peripheral Nervous System (PNS): The PNS includes all the nerves outside the CNS, extending throughout the body to transmit signals between the CNS and the limbs, organs, and tissues. It is further divided into the somatic nervous system and the autonomic nervous system.

- **Somatic Nervous System**: The somatic nervous system controls voluntary movements and sensory perception, allowing us to interact with the external environment. It consists of sensory neurons that transmit signals from sensory receptors to the CNS and motor neurons that convey signals from the CNS to muscles, enabling voluntary movements.

- **Autonomic Nervous System** (ANS): The autonomic nervous system regulates involuntary bodily functions such as heart rate, digestion, respiratory rate, and glandular secretion. It operates automatically, without conscious control, to maintain homeostasis and respond to internal and external stimuli. The ANS is further subdivided into the sympathetic nervous system and the parasympathetic nervous system.

- **Sympathetic Nervous System**: The sympathetic nervous system is responsible for activating the body's "fight or flight" response in response to perceived threats or stressors. It increases heart rate, dilates airways, and redirects blood flow to essential organs to prepare the body for action.

- **Parasympathetic Nervous System**: The parasympathetic nervous system opposes the effects of the sympathetic nervous system, promoting relaxation, rest, and digestion. It slows heart rate, constricts airways, and enhances digestive functions during periods of rest and recovery.

Together, the central and peripheral nervous systems work in concert to regulate bodily functions, maintain homeostasis, and enable complex behaviors and responses to the environment. The nervous system is essential for survival and plays a crucial role in all aspects of human experience, from sensation and movement to cognition and emotion.

The nervous system acts as a central mediator in achieving the goals of self-care, facilitating physical, mental, and emotional health, and promoting a balanced and fulfilling life. It lies at the very heart of our ability to handle life's challenges with resilience and grace. Sweetwater Health describes the difference between the two aspects of the Autonomic system like this: *"The sympathetic and parasympathetic nervous systems act like the accelerator and brakes on a car. The sympathetic system is the accelerator, always ready to rev up and take us out of danger. The parasympathetic system is the brakes, slowing us down when danger isn't present."* The sympathetic nervous system is often referred to as the "fight or flight" response. In our modern day world, where stressors can often overwhelm, it is very common for people to get stuck in this "fight or flight" response, even when they are engaging in relaxing or enjoyable behaviors. This creates a unique situation where burnout, adrenal fatigue, and a whole host of physical, emotional, and physiological symptoms arise to indicate things are out of balance.

Many things can lead to chronic activation of the sympathetic nervous system, also known as sympathetic overactivity or dominance. Things to consider as potential problem areas are:

- Chronic Stress (work pressure, relationships, housing or food instability, caregiving responsibilities, financial worries, etc.)
- Poor Sleep Quality (sleep disorders like insomnia or sleep apnea, disruption to sleep from loud noises or urgency/frequency of urination, etc.)
- Unhealthy lifestyle habits (poor diet, lack of exercise, excessive alcohol consumption, smoking/vaping, substance abuse)
- Sedentary Lifestyle (prolonged periods of sitting or minimal physical activity)
- Chronic Pain (chronic back pain, migraines, fibromyalgia, arthritis, etc. can trigger sympathetic nervous system activation)
- Medical Conditions (hypertension, heart disease, diabetes, obesity, hyperthyroidism, anxiety disorders etc.)
- Environmental factors (noise or air pollution, extreme temperatures, overcrowded or unhygienic living conditions)
- Psychological Factors (anxiety, depression, trauma, mental health issues)
- Caffeine and Stimulant Use (overuse of coffee, tea, soda, energy drinks, and some weight loss pills)

- Medications (certain medications like decongestants, bron-
chodilators, asthma medications, thyroid hormone and
some anti-depressants)

Studies show that between 50-80% of workers experience
burnout and that it can negatively affect all areas of their
life. Burnout and overwhelm are so common post-pandemic,
that the World Health Organization (WHO) has recognized
occupational stress as a major contributor to health issues. It's
easy to see how chronic stress can impact sleep quality, leading
to an increase in stimulant use to get through the day. When
you're amped up on stimulants, you can get edgy and impatient,
making you more snappy and discontent with co-workers
and loved ones. It becomes an endless cycle that many try
to manage with drugs, alcohol, and medications; all of which
numb and disconnect you from the reality of the situation and
the self-awareness that is necessary to make real change.

Since the primary goal of self-care is to regulate the nervous
system and ensure that all systems are functioning optimally,
building awareness around how we are currently living our
lives is an important first step. For individuals who are
stuck in a "fight or flight" response, it becomes enormously
important to begin this self-care journey by focusing on
this first section on nervous system regulation to ensure
there is proper modulation between the sympathetic and
parasympathetic nervous systems. Once you're able to down-
regulate your nervous system, other forms of self-care will
"stick" and you will feel the benefit from them more fully.

This collection isn't meant to cover every possible option,
and there's no pressure to try everything. Instead, consider it
a starting point: read through the suggestions and choose the

ones that resonate with you. If you have physical constraints, breathwork can be a great initial step.

Deep Breathing Exercises

Breathwork is the intentional practice of controlling the breath. It has a profound effect on the nervous system by balancing and modulating its function. Certain types of breathwork can stimulate the parasympathetic nervous system to encourage the relaxation response, which promotes feelings of calmness, relaxation, and overall feelings of well-being. While you can also use breathwork to activate the sympathetic nervous system (which is a great tool to use before taking an exam or giving a presentation to increase alertness), we will be focusing on the former to promote feelings of calm.

- **Diaphragmatic breathing (belly breathing):** Sit or lie down comfortably. Place one hand on your chest and the other on your abdomen. Inhale deeply through your nose, allowing your abdomen to rise as you fill your lungs with air. Exhale slowly through your mouth, feeling your abdomen fall. Repeat for several breaths, focusing on the sensation of your breath filling your belly.
- **478 Breathing:** Inhale deeply through your nose for a count of 4. Hold your breath for a count of 7. Exhale slowly and completely through your mouth for a count of 8. Repeat this cycle several times, focusing on the rhythm of your breath.
- **Box Breathing (or square breathing):** Inhale deeply through your nose for a count of 4. Hold your breath for a count of 4. Exhale slowly through your mouth for a count of 4. Hold your breath for a count of 4. Repeat this

cycle several times, visualizing each side of a square as you breathe.

- **Alternate Nostril Breathing (Nadi Shodhana):** Sit comfortably with your spine straight. Use your right thumb to close your right nostril and inhale deeply through your left nostril. At the top of your inhale, use your right ring finger to close your left nostril and exhale through your right nostril. Inhale through your right nostril, then switch fingers to exhale through your left nostril. Continue this alternating pattern for several breaths, focusing on the flow of air and balancing your breath.

- **Equal Breathing (Sama Vritti):** Inhale through your nose for a count of 4. Exhale through your nose for a count of 4. Keep the inhale and exhale equal in length. Focus on the steady rhythm of your breath to promote relaxation and balance.

- **Guided Imagery Breathing:** Close your eyes and imagine a peaceful scene or place where you feel relaxed and safe. As you inhale deeply, visualize yourself breathing in calmness, peace, or healing energy. As you exhale slowly, imagine releasing tension, stress, or negativity from your body and mind.

- **3-Part Breath (Dirga Pranayama):** Sit comfortably with your spine straight. Inhale deeply through your nose, sequentially filling your belly, rib cage, and chest with air. Exhale slowly and completely through your nose, reversing the process by emptying your chest, rib cage, and belly. Repeat this three-part breath cycle several times, focusing on the smooth transition between each stage.

- **Humming Bee Breath (Bhramari Pranayama):** Close

your eyes and sit comfortably. Inhale deeply through your nose. As you exhale, gently press your thumbs against your ears to close them, and lightly place your fingers over your eyes. With your mouth closed, exhale slowly while making a humming sound like a bee. Feel the vibration in your head and chest as you continue to hum. Repeat several times, focusing on the calming effect of the sound and breath.

- **Ocean Breath (Ujjayi Pranayama):** Sit comfortably with your spine straight. Inhale deeply through your nose, slightly constricting the back of your throat to create a soft hissing or ocean-like sound. Exhale slowly through your nose while maintaining the constriction in the throat. Continue this deep, steady breathing pattern, focusing on the sound and sensation of the breath.

- **Extended Exhale Breathing:** Inhale deeply through your nose for a count of 4. Exhale slowly and completely through your mouth for a count of 6 or 8. Focus on extending the length of your exhale to promote relaxation and activate the parasympathetic nervous system.

- **Visualization Breathing:** Close your eyes and visualize a peaceful scene or object in your mind's eye. As you inhale deeply, imagine drawing in the essence of this peaceful image or energy. As you exhale slowly, visualize releasing any tension, stress, or negativity from your body and mind. Repeat this visualization with each breath, allowing yourself to become more deeply relaxed with each exhale.

- **Counting Breath:** Inhale deeply through your nose for a count of 4. Hold your breath at the top for a count of 4. Exhale slowly and completely through your nose for a count of 4. Hold your breath at the bottom for a count of 4.

Repeat this cycle, counting each inhale, hold, exhale, and hold, focusing on the rhythmic pattern of your breath and counting to maintain awareness and regulate the nervous system.

- **Belly to Chest Breathing:** Lie down comfortably on your back with one hand on your belly and the other on your chest. Inhale deeply through your nose, allowing your belly to rise first and then your chest. Exhale slowly through your mouth, letting your chest fall first and then your belly. Focus on the sensation of your breath moving through your body and the gentle rise and fall of your hands.

- **Sighing Breath:** Inhale deeply through your nose, filling your lungs with air. Exhale audibly through your mouth, releasing a long, audible sigh. Repeat this several times, allowing each sigh to release tension and promote relaxation in the body and mind.

Vagus Nerve Activation

The vagus nerve is the tenth cranial nerve and one of the longest and most important nerves in the body. It originates in the brainstem and extends down the sides of the neck, through the chest and abdomen, and branches out to various organs throughout the body. It plays a very crucial role in the regulation of many essential bodily functions, including heart rate, digestion, respiratory rate, and the functioning of several organs. When activated, it triggers a "rest and digest" phenomenon where the body conserves energy, relaxes the body, and allows for recovery from stress. By employing some simple vagal nerve stimulation techniques, we can intentionally tap into this response to help our nervous systems reset during times of stress. Here are some techniques you can try and see what works for your body.

- **Gargling:** Gargling water or mouthwash can stimulate the gag reflex, which activates the vagus nerve. Gargle for 30 seconds, focusing your energy on the back of your throat
- **Singing or chanting:** Singing or chanting involves controlled breathing and vocalization which can stimulate the vagus nerve. Sing along to your favorite songs or practice chanting mantras or affirmations. My personal favorite is the Gayatri Mantra by Deva Premal
- **Humming:** Humming can stimulate the vagus nerve by activating the muscles in the back of the throat. Humming to a song or just humming on your breath out works in the same way.
- **Tapping/Vibration:** Tapping or using a vibrating device along the clavicle or neck area can stimulate the vagus nerve
- **Cold Exposure:** Brief exposure to cold water, such as cold showers, splashing your face with cold water, or using a cold water plunge tank, stimulates the vagus nerve and promotes relaxation through the receptors in the skin. Ending your shower with a brief blast of cold water can help prepare you for your day.
- **Laughter:** Laughter triggers the release of endorphins and stimulates the vagus nerve. Watch a funny movie, listen to a comedy show, or practice laughter yoga (yes, it's a real thing). Or challenge a friend to the "small smile" game where you compete to make the smallest smile. Invariably, you will both start laughing.
- **Chewing:** Chewing gum or eating crunchy foods can

stimulate the vagus nerve through the act of mastication. Chew slowly and mindfully to maximize benefits at every meal.

- **Acupuncture or acupressure:** targeting specific points to affect the vagus nerve can be an effective strategy to down-regulate the nervous system
- **Wearable Devices:** Studies have found that certain wearable devices that monitor heart rate variability can provide helpful biofeedback to train individuals to self-regulate
- **Vagus Nerve Stimulation Devices:** Some devices stimulate the vagus nerve through electrical stimulation. Ensure the device is approved by your healthcare professional for your situation.
- **Massage:** Gentle massage techniques like lymphatic drainage, Swedish effleurage, or craniosacral can trigger stimulation of the vagus nerve and promote relaxation
- **Orgasm:** Whether by yourself or with a partner, the post-orgasmic sensation is a complete reset of the nervous system

Drink Relaxing Teas

The following teas have properties that support overall relaxation and well-being and are known for their calming and soothing effects:

- **Chamomile Tea:** Chamomile tea is well-known for its calming properties. It is often used to promote relaxation and relieve stress and anxiety. By promoting a sense of calmness and relaxation, it may indirectly support vagal tone.
- **Peppermint Tea:** Peppermint tea has a refreshing and

invigorating aroma and may help soothe digestive discomfort. While there isn't direct evidence linking peppermint tea to vagal tone, promoting digestive health may indirectly support overall well-being.

- **Lemon Balm Tea:** Lemon balm is a member of the mint family. It has traditionally been used to promote relaxation and reduce stress and anxiety. Drinking lemon balm tea may help calm the nervous system and promote relaxation.
- **Lavender Tea:** Lavender is known for its calming and soothing properties and is often used in aromatherapy to promote relaxation. Drinking lavender tea may help reduce stress and anxiety and promote a sense of calmness.
- **Valerian Root Tea:** Valerian root is a popular herbal remedy for promoting relaxation and improving sleep quality. While more research is needed, some studies suggest valerian root may help support the nervous system and promote relaxation.
- **Passionflower Tea:** Passionflower is a vine native to North America. It has traditionally been used to promote relaxation and reduce anxiety. Drinking passionflower tea may help calm the mind and promote relaxation.

Mindfulness Meditation

Mindfulness meditation is a practice that cultivates present-moment awareness, allowing individuals to observe their thoughts, feelings, and sensations with openness and acceptance. By intentionally directing attention to the present moment without judgment, mindfulness meditation helps to quiet the mind, reduce stress, and promote overall well-being. Research has shown that regular mindfulness meditation practice can have profound effects on both mental and physical health, including reducing symptoms of anxiety and depression, improving sleep quality, enhancing focus and concentration, and even boosting immune function. As a powerful tool for self-awareness and self-regulation, mindfulness meditation offers a pathway to greater resilience, emotional balance, and a deeper sense of connection with oneself and the world around us.

- **Breath Awareness Meditation:** Focuses on observing the breath as it moves in and out of the body. Practitioners pay attention to the sensations of the breath without trying to control it, using the breath as an anchor for their attention.
- **Body Scan Meditation:** Involves systematically directing attention to different parts of the body, starting from the toes and moving upward to the head. Practitioners observe sensations, tensions, or areas of discomfort in each body part without judgment, promoting relaxation and awareness.
- **Loving Kindness (Metta) Meditation:** Cultivates feelings of love, compassion, and goodwill toward oneself and others. Practitioners repeat phrases or affirmations wishing themselves and others well-being, happiness, and peace.
- **Walking Meditation:** Involves walking slowly and mindfully, paying attention to each step, sensation, and movement of the body. Practitioners may focus on the sensation of their feet touching the ground or the rhythm of their steps.
- **Body Sensations Meditation:** Explores sensations in the body as they arise in the present moment. Practitioners observe physical sensations such as tingling, warmth, or

tension without reacting to or judging them, fostering greater bodily awareness.

- **Sound Meditation:** Focuses on listening to sounds in the environment with open awareness, without labeling or judging them. Practitioners may notice the qualities of different sounds, such as their pitch, volume, or duration, as they come and go.
- **Visualization Meditation:** Involves mentally picturing a scene, image, or object in the mind's eye. Practitioners may imagine themselves in a peaceful setting or imagine positive outcomes and experiences, fostering relaxation and positive emotions.
- **Open Awareness Meditation:** Cultivates open, non-judgmental awareness of present-moment experiences as they arise. Practitioners observe thoughts, emotions, sensations, and sounds without getting caught up in them or trying to change them, promoting acceptance and clarity.
- **Mantra Meditation:** Involves silently repeating a word, phrase, or sound (mantra) to focus the mind and promote relaxation. Practitioners may choose a traditional mantra or create their own, repeating it with each breath or as a focal point of attention.
- **Body Movement Meditation:** Incorporates gentle movement practices such as yoga, qigong, or tai chi to cultivate mindfulness and awareness of the body's movements, sensations, and breath.

Progressive Muscle Relaxation

Progressive muscle relaxation (PMR) is a relaxation technique designed to reduce muscle tension and promote a sense of calm. It involves systematically tensing and then relaxing different muscle groups in the body, typically beginning from the toes and working upward or vice versa. The process requires focused attention on the feelings of tension and relaxation, helping to increase body awareness and relieve stress. Here's how to practice PMR:

- Find a Comfortable Position: Sit or lie down in a comfortable position, such as on a chair or bed, with your eyes closed and your body relaxed.
- Take a Deep Breath: Begin by taking a few deep breaths to center yourself and bring your awareness to the present moment.
- Progressive Muscle Tensing: Start with a specific muscle group, such as your hands or feet. Tense the muscles in that group as tightly as you can for about 5-10 seconds while maintaining steady breathing.
- Hold the Tension: Hold the tension in the muscles for a few seconds, focusing on the sensation of tightness and tension in that area.
- Release and Relax: Suddenly, release the tension in the muscles and allow them to relax completely. Focus on the sensation of relaxation and the contrast between tension and relaxation in that muscle group.
- Pause and Rest: Take a moment to rest and observe the sensations in the relaxed muscles before moving on to the next muscle group.
- Repeat with Other Muscle Groups: Continue the process of tensing and relaxing different muscle groups in your body, working your way systematically from one muscle group to another. Common muscle groups to focus on

include the hands, arms, shoulders, neck, face, chest, abdomen, buttocks, thighs, calves, and feet.

- Progressive Relaxation from Head to Toe: Alternatively, you can also practice PMR by systematically tensing and relaxing muscle groups from head to toe or vice versa, depending on your preference.
- Practice Regularly: Aim to practice PMR regularly, ideally once or twice a day, to experience its full benefits and build relaxation skills over time.

Yoga

Participate in yoga classes that downregulate the nervous system. As you become more skilled at breathwork and connect breath to poses, you can find the same type of nervous system downregulation in more powerful or active forms of yoga (Ashtanga, Warm Flow, Bikram, Power Yoga, etc.). Below is a list of yoga types that are appropriate for absolute beginners.

- **Restorative Yoga:** Focuses on gentle, supported poses held for extended periods to promote deep relaxation and release tension. Props such as bolsters, blankets, and blocks are often used to provide support and comfort.
- **Yin Yoga:** Involves holding passive poses for several minutes, allowing for deep stretching and the release of tension in the connective tissues. It encourages surrender and acceptance and promotes relaxation and introspection.
- **Yoga Nidra:** Also known as yogic sleep, Yoga Nidra is a guided relaxation practice that induces a state of deep relaxation and conscious sleep. Practitioners lie down in a comfortable position and follow verbal instructions to

38

systematically relax different parts of the body and explore sensations, emotions, and imagery.

- **Meditative Yoga:** Combines gentle movement with mindfulness meditation, encouraging practitioners to cultivate present-moment awareness and inner stillness. Its practices often involve slow, intentional movements synchronized with the breath.

- **Vinyasa or Flow Yoga:** Incorporates slow, fluid movements and gentle transitions between poses to promote relaxation and ease in the body. Seek out a flow class that is either "Gentle Flow" or "Slow Flow," as these typically focus on breath-centered movement and mindful awareness.

- **Gentle Yoga:** Gentle yoga classes are designed to be accessible for practitioners of all ages and fitness levels, including beginners and those with physical limitations or injuries. These classes typically include gentle stretches, simple poses, and breath work to promote relaxation and well-being and will be less focused on flowing consecutively through the poses.

- **Wall Yoga:** Wall Yoga uses the support of a wall to assist with alignment, balance, and stability in yoga poses. It is particularly beneficial for beginners or those with mobility or balance concerns, as the wall acts as a guide to help safely explore postures. You can also leverage the wall to promote proper alignment and deepen the stretch. This practice offers a grounded approach to yoga, making it both accessible and supportive for nervous system regulation and relaxation.

- **Chair Yoga:** Chair yoga offers modifications of traditional yoga poses that can be performed while seated or using a chair for support. It is accessible to beginners, seniors, and individuals with limited mobility or balance issues.

Grounding Techniques

Grounding techniques are practices that help individuals stay centered and connected to the present moment. They are particularly helpful for managing anxiety, stress, or dissociation.

- **Body Scan:** Focus on different parts of your body, starting from your toes and moving upward to your head. Notice any sensations or tension in each part, and consciously relax those muscles as you scan them.
- **Grounding Objects:** Hold onto a physical object, such as a smooth stone, a piece of jewelry, or a stress ball. Pay attention to its texture, weight, and temperature, using it as a point of focus to anchor yourself in the present moment.
- **Visualization:** Imagine yourself as a tree with roots extending deep into the earth, grounding you and providing stability. Visualize these roots growing stronger with each breath, anchoring you securely in the present moment.
- **Name your Emotions:** Label your emotions and acknowledge them without judgment. For example, say to yourself, "I'm feeling anxious right now," or "I'm feeling overwhelmed." Naming your emotions can help you gain clarity and distance from them.
- **Five Senses Exercise:** Engage each of your five senses by actively noticing and describing things in your environment. Describe five things you see, four things you hear, three things you touch, two things you smell, and one thing you taste.
- **Grounding Affirmations:** Repeat grounding affirma-

tions or mantras to yourself, such as "I am safe," "I am present," or "This too shall pass." Choose affirmations that resonate with you and help you feel grounded and centered.

- **Connect with the Earth:** If possible, go outside and walk or lay barefoot on grass, sand, or soil. Feel the sensation of the ground beneath your feet, connecting you to the earth's energy and providing a sense of grounding and stability. There is new scientific research that shows there are measurable benefits to the body by walking, laying on, or otherwise touching elements of the earth. Jumping in a lake, ocean, or river, burying feet in a sandy beach, climbing or hugging a tree, gardening, and simply gazing at a sunrise or sunset can all have a measurable effect on calming the nervous system.

- **Breath Counting:** Focus on counting your breaths, inhaling and exhaling slowly and deliberately. Count each breath silently, starting from one and continuing up to a predetermined number, such as five or ten, then start again from one.

- **Use your Imagination:** Imagine yourself in a safe, calming place, such as a peaceful beach, a serene forest, or a cozy room. Visualize the details of this place in your mind, focusing on the sights, sounds, and **sensations to create a sense of grounding and relaxation.**

Sound Therapy

Sound therapy, also known as sound healing, is a therapeutic practice that uses sound vibrations to improve physical and emotional health and well-being by promoting relaxation and reducing stress. The underlying principle is that sound can influence the body's energy fields and stimulate the brain to induce a meditative state, balance energy, and promote overall well-being.

- **Music Therapy:** Listening to calming music with slow tempos, gentle melodies, and soothing harmonies can help reduce stress and promote relaxation. Genres such as classical, ambient, and nature-inspired music are often used.
- **Binaural Beats:** This technique uses two slightly different frequencies played in each ear, creating a third frequency or "beat" in the brain. Binaural beats can promote relaxation and are often associated with different brainwave states, such as alpha (relaxation) and theta (meditative).
- **Solfeggio Frequencies:** These are a series of specific sound frequencies believed to have various healing properties. They are commonly used in meditation, sound healing, and relaxation practices. They are believed to resonate with our energy centers (chakras) and influence our emotional and physical well-being. Each frequency has a unique effect:

- 396 Hz – Liberating Guilt and Fear - This frequency is said to help release guilt and fear, allowing for emotional healing and a sense of security.
- 417 Hz – Undoing Situations and Facilitating Change - Known for promoting change and transformation, this frequency is believed to help release negative patterns and encourage new beginnings.
- 528 Hz - Transformation and Miracles (DNA Repair) - Often referred to as the "Love Frequency," 528 Hz is linked to positive transformation and is thought to help repair DNA, fostering healing at a cellular level.
- 639 Hz – Connecting/Relationships - This frequency fosters harmonious relationships and promotes understanding, empathy, and love between individuals.
- 741 Hz - Expression/Solutions - Known for stimulating creativity and enhancing problem-solving, 741 Hz promotes self-expression and clear communication.
- 852 Hz – Returning to Spiritual Order - Often associated with awakening intuition and spiritual insight, 852 Hz is believed to encourage alignment with spiritual truths and a deeper connection to higher consciousness.
- 963 Hz – Awakening Perfect State - This frequency is linked to spiritual awakening and enlightenment, often considered the "frequency of the gods." It is said to help connect with universal consciousness and encourage spiritual clarity.

- **Nature Sounds:** Listening to natural sounds like flowing water, birdsong, rain, or ocean waves can create a calming environment that helps the SNS downregulate. These sounds are often used in relaxation and meditation practices.
- **Sound Baths:** In a sound bath, participants lie down while various instruments such as singing bowls, gongs, didgeridoo, chimes, electronic music, or other instruments are played around them. The sound vibrations are thought to promote relaxation and reduce stress through the vibrations they create within the body.
- **Tuning Fork Therapy:** Tuning forks, which produce specific frequencies when struck, are used in various ways to promote relaxation and balance. The vibrations can be applied near or on the body to create calming effects.
- **White Noise:** White noise is a consistent, unobtrusive sound that can mask other background noises. It helps create a calming environment and is often used to promote sleep and reduce stress.
- **Guided Meditations with Sound:** These meditations

combine spoken guidance with calming background sounds or music. The audio guidance helps focus the mind while the sound promotes relaxation.

- **ASMR (Autonomous Sensory Meridian Response):** Some people find relaxation through specific sounds or stimuli, such as whispering, tapping, or gentle rustling. ASMR videos and recordings are can be accessed online to trigger a calming response.
- **Chanting and Mantras:** Repeating calming words or sounds, such as "Om," can help focus the mind and create a sense of peace. Chanting is often used in meditation and yoga practices to promote relaxation.
- **Aromatherapy:** You can access the healing properties of plants through inhalation, topical application, or soaking in a bath infused with aromatic essential oils. These have been used for centuries to alleviate anxiety and stress and promote relaxation.
- **Lavender:** Known for its calming and soothing properties, lavender is widely used to reduce stress and promote relaxation.
- **Chamomile:** Both Roman and German chamomile have calming effects that can help alleviate stress and anxiety.
- **Frankincense:** This essential oil has grounding properties and can help promote a sense of calm.
- **Bergamot:** With its citrus aroma, bergamot has mood-lifting and stress-relieving effects.
- **Ylang Ylang:** This sweet and floral oil is known for its ability to calm nerves and reduce stress.
- **Sandalwood:** Sandalwood has a warm, woody scent that is often used to promote relaxation and reduce anxiety.
- **Clary Sage:** This oil has a calming effect on the mind and

body, making it useful for reducing stress and promoting relaxation.

- **Rose:** Rose oil has a calming fragrance and is known for reducing stress and promoting emotional balance.
- **Patchouli:** With its earthy aroma, patchouli can help promote relaxation and reduce tension.
- **Neroli:** This citrusy oil is known for its calming properties and can help alleviate anxiety.

Limit Stimulants

Stimulants are substances that increase activity in the central nervous system, often resulting in heightened alertness, energy and focus. While they can have beneficial effects when used appropriately, excessive or prolonged use can lead to over stimulation of the nervous system, potentially causing adverse effects.

- **Caffeine:** Found in coffee, tea, energy drinks, and some medications, caffeine is one of the most widely consumed stimulants. Excessive caffeine intake can lead to jitteriness, anxiety, insomnia, and rapid heartbeat.
- **Nicotine:** Found in tobacco products such as cigarettes, cigars, and vaping devices, nicotine stimulates the release of adrenaline and dopamine, leading to increased alertness and pleasure. However, nicotine can also cause increased heart rate, elevated blood pressure, and dependence.
- **Amphetamines:** Prescription medications such as Adderall and Ritalin, commonly used to treat attention deficit hyperactivity disorder (ADHD), are central nervous system stimulants. While they can improve focus and attention in individuals with ADHD, misuse or abuse of these drugs can

lead to nervousness, agitation, insomnia, and addiction.

- **Synthetic Cathinones (Bath Salts):** These synthetic stimulants are chemically similar to amphetamines and produce effects such as increased energy, alertness, and euphoria. However, they can also cause agitation, paranoia, hallucinations, and cardiovascular complications.
- **Energy Drinks:** Beverages containing high levels of caffeine, sugar, and other stimulants can provide a temporary energy boost but may also lead to jitteriness, anxiety, insomnia, and rapid heartbeat, especially when consumed in excess.
- **Prescription Stimulants:** In addition to amphetamines used to treat ADHD, other prescription medications such as certain antidepressants, decongestants, and weight loss drugs can have stimulant effects and may cause nervousness, agitation, and other nervous system disturbances.
- **Illicit Stimulants:** Various other illicit drugs, such as crack cocaine, khat, MDMA (molly or Ecstacy), Methamphetamine (meth), and synthetic cathinones (e.g., flakka), can act as potent stimulants and may disrupt the nervous system, leading to adverse effects on mood, behavior, and cognition.

Journal

Journaling is a form of self-exploration, self-reflection, and self-discovery. By writing down your thoughts, feelings, experiences, and reflections in a journal or notebook, you create a space to integrate information and process life events. It is also helpful for tracking progress on goals or gaining insights into patterns of behavior. It can be a therapeutic tool for downregulating the nervous system, alleviating stress, solving problems, and promoting relaxation, especially when specific techniques are utilized.

- **Gratitude Journaling:** Write down three things you're grateful for each day. Focusing on positive aspects of your life can shift your mindset toward gratitude, promoting feelings of contentment and well-being.
- **Emotion Journaling:** Express and explore your emotions by writing about how you're feeling. Describe the emotions you're experiencing, their triggers, and any physical sensations associated with them. This process can help you process and release pent-up emotions, promoting emotional regulation.
- **Stream-of-Consciousness Writing:** Set a timer for a specific duration (e.g., 10-15 minutes) and write continuously without pausing or censoring your thoughts. Let your mind wander, and write down whatever comes to mind, even if it seems random or nonsensical. This free-flowing writing style can help release mental clutter and promote relaxation.
- **Reflection Journaling:** Take time to reflect on your day, experiences, or interactions. Write about what went well, what you learned, and how you'd like to approach similar situations in the future. Reflective journaling can promote self-awareness, insight, and personal growth.
- **Mindfulness Journaling:** Use your journal as a tool for mindfulness by writing about your present-moment experiences. Describe your surroundings, sensations, thoughts, and emotions with curiosity and nonjudgmental awareness. Mindful journaling can help you stay grounded and present, reducing stress and promoting relaxation.

- **Self-Compassion Journaling:** Practice self-compassion by writing yourself a compassionate letter or journal entry. Acknowledge any struggles or challenges you're facing with kindness and understanding. Offer yourself words of comfort, support, and encouragement, fostering self-compassion and self-soothing.
- **Visualization Journaling:** Write about your ideal future or visualize a peaceful, calming scene in detail. Describe the sights, sounds, smells, and sensations of this imagined experience. Visualization journaling can evoke feelings of relaxation, optimism, and hopefulness.
- **Creative Expression Journaling:** Use your journal as a space for creative expression through writing, drawing, painting, or collage. Allow yourself to explore and express your thoughts, feelings, and experiences in whatever medium feels most natural and authentic to you.
- **ZenTangles/Doodle Journaling:** Zentangle journaling combines the meditative practice of Zentangle drawing with journaling to promote relaxation, creativity, and self-expression. Zentangle is a method of creating intricate, abstract drawings using repetitive patterns and deliberate strokes.
- **Affirmation Journaling:** Write down positive affirmations or self-affirming statements that resonate with you. Repeat these affirmations daily or whenever you need a confidence boost or reminder of your inner strength and resilience.

Express Emotions

- **Talk to Someone:** Share your feelings with a trusted

friend, family member, or therapist. Talking about your emotions can help you process them and gain perspective. If you have trouble being vulnerable with family or friends and the thought of talk therapy is unnerving, try working with a process coach. A process coach will help guide you through your emotions with a variety of exercises in a safe and comfortable space.

- **Allow yourself to Cry:** Allow yourself to cry if you feel the need. Crying can be a natural and cathartic way to release intense emotions and relieve emotional pressure.
- **Engage in Creative Expression:** Express your emotions through creative outlets such as art, music, dance, or poetry. Allow yourself to explore and express your feelings without judgment or inhibition.
- **Scream or Shout:** Find a private space to safely release pent-up emotions by screaming or shouting into a pillow or a secluded outdoor area. Letting out a primal scream can provide temporary relief and release.
- **Engage in Cathartic Activities:** These activities allow for physical release, such as punching a pillow, tearing paper, or smashing clay. They can provide a safe and healthy outlet for releasing anger or frustration.
- **Explore Emotional Release Techniques:** Explore specific techniques designed to release stored emotional energy, such as Emotional Freedom Techniques (EFT), also known as tapping, or Eye Movement Desensitization and Reprocessing (EMDR).

3

PHYSICAL SELF-CARE

"Take care of your body. It's the only place you have to live." - Jim Rohn

T he human body is remarkably resilient and self-reliant. It doesn't require conscious thought to ensure that our lungs fill with oxygen or transfer it to the blood so the heart can pump it throughout the system. But that doesn't mean our bodies should be ignored. There are many things we can do to support their optimal functioning and maximize the number of quality, enjoyable years we can experience.

Self-care for physical health involves taking deliberate steps to prioritize and maintain your physical well-being. This affects all activities that nourish, energize, and rejuvenate your body. This includes what foods/substances/liquids we allow into our bodies, how we use/move our bodies, how we maintain the cleanliness of our bodies, and how we approach seeking preventative and emergency medical care. Much of the activities in physical self-care are habituated into a daily or weekly routine for ongoing maintenance and, as such, are overlooked as essential forms of self-care.

Many of these will be common sense or already a part of your daily/weekly routines. That's great. Celebrate what you're doing well. If you know you struggle with a particular category of physical self-care (a common one is hydration), see if any of the tips speak to you as something to explore. Sometimes, simply setting daily/weekly/monthly/yearly notifications or reminders into your calendar or clock can provide the awareness necessary to take more consistent action. Experiment and play to expand your successes!

Hydrate

- Drink ½ to 1 ounce of water daily for every pound you weigh. For example, if you weigh 150 pounds, drink 75 to 150 ounces (or roughly 2 ½ to 4 ½ liters daily).
- Set timers on your watch, phone, or computer for regular breaks to get up, move, stretch, and hydrate.
- Increase awareness of muscle tightness and early signs of muscle cramping. Add electrolytes to water to ensure your body uses the water you drink optimally.
- Build a habit of bringing a reusable bottle with you wherever you go.
- Drink a glass of water before each meal to aid digestion and feel full before eating.
- Track hydration levels in a journal or app to build awareness and reach hydration goals.
- Add slices of fruits, herbs, or flavor drops to encourage drinking.
- Experiment with your experience regarding water tem-

perature preferences. Would you drink more if the water was room temperature, cooled in the refrigerator, or on ice?

- Set goals around additional types of non-caffeinated hydration, such as herbal teas, coconut water, or sparkling water. Experiment with "rewarding" yourself with one of these hydration treats every time you finish 32 ounces of water.
- Monitor urine color as a hydration indicator. Aim for pale yellow to clear color.
- Limit caffeine and alcohol intake due to their diuretic effect. It works against hydration.
- Drink a glass of lemon water when you first wake up to aid with detoxification.
- Drink chamomile tea before bed to promote relaxation and winding down.
- Invest in a Soda Stream or similar water carbonation device. Adding bubbles to regular water can make it more fun to drink.
- Incorporate fruits and vegetables with high water content into your diet. Examples include cucumbers, celery, tomatoes, oranges, apples, and watermelon.
- Use an app to track your daily hydration. Monitoring consumption helps build awareness and creates a feedback loop to motivate and reward progress.
- Keep a refillable water bottle with you wherever you go. Please make this a non-negotiable so that with time, it becomes a part of your routine when exiting your house (keys, wallet, sunglasses, water bottle, etc.)
- Increase awareness of what limits your water intake. Experiment with various water bottles or glass types.

Some people drink more when they don't have to unscrew a bottle top.

- Experiment with straws. Some people find that the convenience of water bottles with a fixed straw significantly increases their water consumption.

Diet

- Prepare healthy meals at home. One-pot meals or meal prep in advance can help achieve this goal.
- Be mindful of portion size.
- Incorporate more fruits and vegetables into your diet.
- Practice shopping on the grocery store's perimeter for natural, whole-food choices.
- Limit processed foods, dairy, sugar, and sodium intake.
- Limit how much you eat out at restaurants or pick up food on the road. Pack your lunch or eat meals at home.
- Ensure you have healthy snacks like nuts, seeds, or fruit readily available.
- Experiment with new recipes.
- Experiment with trying new vegetables. Our taste buds change as we age. You might be surprised that you love something you used to hate.
- To become more aware of your eating habits (time, quantity, type), you can keep a food journal or track them using an app.
- Commit to a limited daily eating window to give your digestive system a break. Intermittent fasting is an excellent dietary reset tool.
- Refrain from eating after 7 pm to protect quality sleep.

- Practice mindful eating by savoring each bite.
- Pay attention to hunger and fullness cues.
- Eat until you are 80% full, then stop. Wait 20 minutes before eating any more. Studies show that octogenarians worldwide do this, and it leads to a longer life.
- Be mindful of emotional triggers that lead to unhealthy eating patterns. Build alternative coping and soothing strategies that don't involve food.
- Eat food and take supplements to support a healthy gut biome.

Hygiene

- Brush your teeth at least twice daily and floss daily to maintain oral health and prevent gum disease. Using mouthwash can also help reduce bacteria and freshen your breath.
- Showering or bathing at least once a day helps remove dirt, sweat, and bacteria. It's also essential after exercise or any activity that causes sweating.
- Wash your hair regularly to remove dirt and excess oils. The frequency can depend on your hair type and personal needs.
- Wash your feet daily, especially between the toes, and dry them thoroughly to prevent fungal infections. Wear clean socks and ensure your shoes are not damp inside.
- Create a consistent facial hygiene routine. If you wear makeup, remove it before bed to prevent skin irritation and breakouts. Wash your face at least twice a day to keep it clean.
- Use deodorant or antiperspirant to help manage body odor

and reduce sweating. Find one that works well with your body chemistry.

- Trim, shape, and clean fingers and toenails regularly. This prevents the buildup of dirt and bacteria and reduces the risk of nail infections.
- Dry brush your skin before showering/bathing to aid in detoxification.
- Wash your hands regularly. This is the most effective way to prevent the spread of germs. Use soap and water for at least 20 seconds, especially before eating, after using the restroom, and when you come home.
- To avoid foodborne illnesses, practice safe food hygiene. Always wash your hands before handling food, and keep kitchen surfaces clean.
- Wear clean clothes daily and change them after sweating heavily or getting dirty. This is crucial for personal cleanliness and to avoid body odor.
- Clean and disinfect all the doorknobs, light switches, and handles in your house (including the microwave, washer, dryer, faucets, and toilet levers). This will protect your body from unnecessary exposure.
- Organize and declutter living spaces daily so it doesn't stack up and become a chore.
- To prevent bacterial buildup, regularly clean and disinfect personal items such as phones, glasses, and reusable water containers.
- Wash your hands after handling pets, raw meats, or chemicals.
- Practice Safe Sex to prevent sexually transmitted diseases.
- Employ preventative practices to protect overall physical health, including using sunscreen daily and monitoring

for good posture.

Movement/Fitness

- Move your body daily - Consider a step tracker and set goals for movement.
- If you have a fitness watch, connect with friends and set healthy competition/accountability to achieve daily movement goals.
- Get outside to play with your kids.
- Take the stairs whenever you have the option.
- Join an adult sports league for baseball, softball, volleyball, basketball, tennis, etc.
- Incorporate light activities into your routine, like gardening, bird watching, or visiting your surrounding cities' botanical gardens.
- Volunteer at a local retirement home to share the benefits of getting sunlight on the skin with individuals who use wheelchairs.
- Go on local hikes.
- Join a fitness club. You can run, jog, walk, hike, bike, pickleball, or play tennis.
- Lift weights or do bodyweight exercises at home.
- Incorporate resistance band exercises into your workouts.
- To increase mobility and range of motion, attend yoga, tai chi, or other fluid movement classes.
- To build cardiovascular health, take a fitness dance class, such as hip hop, Zumba, barre, belly dancing, pole dancing, salsa, Bollywood, or line dancing.
- Place yourself in a static plank hold. Build up to 30 seconds, 1 minute, 5 minutes, etc. Set goals and watch yourself get

stronger and more confident.

- See if you can do a pull-up. If you can, how many can you do? Set goals and watch yourself quickly improve. If you can't, use a chair to lift yourself into the position and slowly try to release your body weight to a hang. Then, hang and engage the muscles for 5 seconds as if you were going to do a pull-up.
- See if you can do pushups. If you can, how many can you do? Set goals and watch yourself get stronger over time. If you can't, set yourself in the highest position and try to lower down slowly. You can place your knees on the ground or extend them in a plank position. Repeat until you can do a single push-up.
- Time yourself for a one-mile walk, jog, or run. Set goals and watch yourself improve over the course of a month.
- Commit to taking the stairs whenever you have the option.

Body Care Treatments

- Release tight muscles by stretching, using foam rollers, or other body rolling devices.
- To dig into tight spots, use tennis or lacrosse balls and place them under your body weight on the ground or against a wall. Breathe deeply to release knots.
- Get a massage.
- Try a bodywork modality geared toward energy work, such as craniosacral therapy, reiki, polarity, Bowen, or qigong. See if these subtle techniques work better for your body.
- Utilize a Gua Sha tool to stripe muscles and release tension.
- Get Acupressure, Acupuncture, or Cupping Therapy to address energy movement along the body's meridians.

- Enjoy a jacuzzi, steam room, or sauna (wet, dry, or infrared) for their relaxing and detoxifying.
- Do a foot soak, foot scrub, and deep hydration wrap.
- Do a hand soak, hand scrub, and deep hydration wrap.
- Get a paraffin wax treatment.
- Get a manicure or pedicure.
- Get your hair washed, cut, styled, colored.
- Get a facial or give yourself one at home.
- Apply a face mask to remove toxins and hydrate fully with a moisturizing wrap.
- Invest in good foot insoles.
- Walk barefoot on grass or earth to ground your energy.
- Engage the senses with aroma therapy to reduce stress.

Support Healthy Circadian Rhythms

- Change your bed sheets once 1x week.
- Engage in activities that get you outside to get sun on your skin and make natural vitamin D.
- Do not bring your cell phone or other electronic devices into the bedroom.
- Commit to 1 hour of no screen time before bedtime.
- Commit to a consistent bedtime every night and stick to it.
- Commit to a consistent wake-up time every morning and stick to it.
- Try sleeping with the window cracked to bring fresh air into the room.
- Try sleeping with white noise from a fan or air filter to reduce distractions that could wake you from sleep.
- Consider sleeping with earplugs or an eye mask to protect

your sleep zone.
- Consider investing in blackout curtains to create a dark sleeping environment.
- Consider using a diffuser to disperse lavender essential oil into your bedroom for 15 minutes before sleep.
- Commit to no caffeine after 2 pm (or earlier if you're sensitive).
- Commit to no big meals after 7 pm.
- Limit Alcohol before bed. While it can initially make you feel sleepy, it disrupts sleep patterns.
- Avoid vigorous exercise right before bed, but DO exercise daily to maintain a good night's sleep.
- Utilize Sound therapy with megahertz that supports sleep.
- Engage in deep breathing or meditation exercises before bed.
- Invest in a comfortable and supportive mattress.
- Invest in a pillow that supports your type of sleep position (back, belly, side).
- Eliminate your bladder/bowels before going to bed.
- Limit naps. While short naps can be beneficial, longer naps or naps later in the day can interfere with your ability to fall asleep.
- Keep a diary to track your sleep patterns to increase awareness and establish better habits to improve sleep quality.
- Get plenty of sunlight during the day to regulate your internal clock.
- Limit fluid intake right before bed to minimize the likelihood of waking up for toileting.
- Practice gratitude or pray regularly to flood your body with dopamine/serotonin before sleep.

- Use blue light filters/glasses on electronic devices in the evening.
- Avoid stimulating activities before bed (heated discussions, watching action movies, etc.).
- Keep your bedroom tidy. A clutter-free bedroom has been shown to contribute to a sense of calm and relaxation.
- Limit exposure to stressful situations before bed to keep cortisol levels low.
- If you deal with insomnia or rumination, talk to your subconscious mind. Set boundaries with your subconscious: "Now is not the time for these thoughts. Right now, it is time to sleep. Please respect that, and we can continue this conversation tomorrow." I'm telling you, it works!

Health Care

- Schedule regular dental visits.
- Schedule a yearly physical exam.
- Get regular blood pressure screenings.
- Get yearly cholesterol screenings.
- Get regular screenings for common conditions such as cancer, diabetes, and osteoporosis.
- Schedule a yearly eye exam.
- Schedule a yearly OB/gynecologist appointment.
- Do regular self-exams to screen for cancer.
- Quit smoking/vaping.
- Maintain a healthy weight and get support if needed. This will significantly reduce your risk for many diseases.
- Manage chronic conditions with a medical plan.
- Stay current with recommended vaccinations to prevent infectious diseases such as influenza, pneumonia, tetanus,

and HPV.
- Take supplements to support your specific health concerns.
- Perform regular lymphatic drainage techniques or detox protocols to keep your system in tip-top shape.
- Consider seeing a Naturopathic Doctor, Traditional Chinese Medical Doctor, Ayurvedic, Homeopathic, or Holistic Health Practitioner as a complement to Western Medicine.
- Consider seeing a mental health doctor for additional support in achieving your health-related goals. Chronic stress from past trauma, PTSD, depression, anxiety, and substance abuse all affect your physical health but can have components tied to mental health.

Take Health and Wellness Assessments

- Health Risk Assessment (HRA)
- Stress Management Assessment
- Sleep Quality Assessment
- Nutrition and Diet Assessments

Journal Prompts for Physical Health and Well-Being

- How would I describe my current physical health and well-being?
- What physical activities or exercises do I enjoy, and how often do I engage in them?
- What are my biggest challenges or obstacles to maintaining a healthy lifestyle?
- What does a typical day of eating look like, and how do I feel about these dietary habits?
- How well do I prioritize sleep and rest in my daily routine?

- What are my beliefs about my body, and how do they influence my behavior?
- What physical symptoms or discomforts do I experience regularly, and how do they impact my life?
- How do I manage stress and its effects on my physical health?
- What preventive measures do I take to maintain my physical health, such as regular check-ups or screenings?
- What self-care practices do I incorporate into my daily routine to support my physical well-being?
- How do I stay hydrated throughout the day, and what are my typical beverage choices?
- What strategies do I use to manage chronic conditions or health concerns?
- What motivates me to prioritize my physical health, and how do I stay committed to my goals?
- How do I handle setbacks in my journey towards better physical health?
- What role do relaxation and stress management play in supporting my physical well-being?
- What habits or behaviors do I want to change or improve to enhance my physical health?
- Beyond structured exercise sessions, how do I incorporate movement and activity into my daily life?
- What role does nutrition play in my health, and how can I choose healthier food?
- How do I track my progress toward physical health goals, and what milestones have I achieved?
- How do I celebrate when I care for my physical health and well-being?

4

MENTAL SELF-CARE

"You are worth the quiet moment. You are worth the deeper breath. You are worth the time it takes to slow down, be still, and rest." - Morgan Harper Nichols

Mental self-care involves diverse activities and habits designed to support cognitive, emotional, and psychological resilience while honoring each individual's unique challenges and needs. In modern times, the proactive and intentional pursuit of mental well-being has become more normalized, helping to reduce the stigma once associated with seeking mental health support. With a host of low-cost, app-based mental health professionals at your fingertips, supporting and enhancing your mental health has never been easier. Nearly all categories of self-care track back to mental well-being, so the simple act of attempting to balance one's self-care routines as a whole is beneficial to one's mental health.

Self-Inventory

Taking a self-inventory of your current mental health helps to proactively identify and assess concerns, patterns, or symptoms that could be the underlying cause of stress. Through self-reflection and self-awareness practices, individuals can gain insight into their thoughts, feelings, and behaviors, as well as the connections those areas may have with other aspects of life. Since self-care seeks to balance all aspects of a person, mental health screenings and assessments become a powerful tool that can benefit any individual. There are a wide variety of tools and resources available online to conduct personal assessments in the privacy of your own home, and they can be highly enlightening. Ideally, seek out the guidance and support of a licensed therapist for specific concerns.

Attachment Style

Attachment theory, developed by psychologist John Bowlby, describes the psychological and emotional bonds that develop with our caregivers during infancy and childhood. These early attachment experiences can shape the patterns of behavior, emotional regulation, and interpersonal relationships we develop throughout our adult life. Unhealthy patterns that repeat themselves due to unconscious attachment conditioning have the potential to sabotage our ability to make meaningful connections with others and access intimacy/vulnerability in a way that feels safe. If we're cut off from deep and meaningful social connections, we are at risk for isolation, loneliness, anxiety, depression, and other adverse health issues. Learning your attachment style gives you a framework to address behavioral adjustments and unconscious repatterning so you can connect more deeply with others. It also gives you the tools to be more compassionate and understanding with friends and family's behaviors. When you see these patterns in others, you can also show up more lovingly for them.

Understand the Four Attachment styles

1. Secure attachment: Individuals with a secure attachment style feel comfortable with intimacy and independence. They trust their caregivers to be responsive and available when needed, allowing them to explore the world confidently. As adults, they tend to form secure, stable relationships characterized by trust, communication, and emotional support. They can rely on themselves or others to meet their needs and are generally open, vulnerable, and intimate.

2. Anxious-preoccupied attachment: People with an anxious-preoccupied attachment style crave intimacy and fear abandonment but may doubt their self-worth or the reliability of their caregivers. They often seek reassurance and validation from others, experiencing heightened anxiety and insecurity in relationships. They may worry about rejection or abandonment and exhibit clingy or demanding behaviors to maintain closeness. They can't rely on themselves to meet their own needs and believe they must rely on others to get those needs met, which results in the impression of being clingy and dependent on others.

3. Dismissive-avoidant attachment: Individuals with a dismissive-avoidant attachment style value independence

and self-reliance over intimacy and emotional connection. They may suppress or downplay their emotions and avoid getting too close to others to protect themselves from potential hurt or rejection. They may appear distant or aloof in relationships, preferring to maintain a sense of autonomy and detachment. They rely on themselves to meet their needs because they don't believe others can be trusted to meet them or show up consistently. This often leads to hyper-independence and self-reliance.

4. Fearful-avoidant attachment (also known as disorganized attachment): People with a fearful-avoidant attachment style experience conflicting desires for intimacy and independence, often due to past experiences of trauma or abuse. They may oscillate between seeking closeness and withdrawing from relationships out of fear of rejection or harm. They may struggle with trust issues, emotional volatility, and difficulty forming or maintaining stable relationships. They don't believe they can trust themselves or others to meet their needs, so the world tends to feel unsafe and challenging to navigate. They often have low self-esteem and high attachment anxiety, which can result in clingy or avoidant behaviors in different situations.

Determine your Attachment style

To quickly determine your attachment style, ask yourself the following two questions, then look at the image below to see which style most aligns with your worldview.

- Do you have a positive or negative view of yourself?
- Do you have a positive or negative view of others?

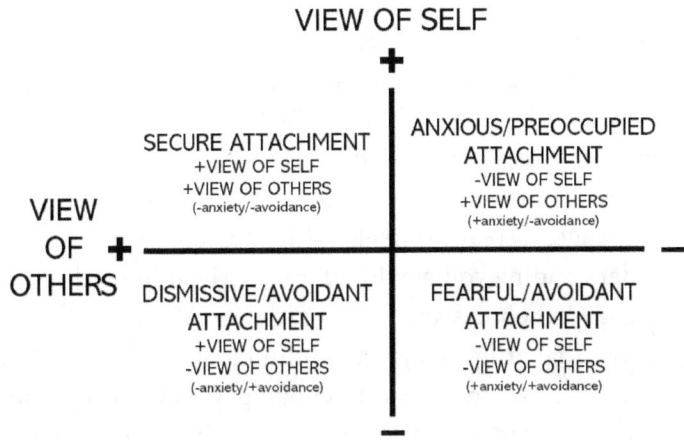

Then, work toward a Secure attachment style by building trust, resilience, and a sense of security in your relationships with yourself and others. Your attachment style isn't your destiny!

- **Dismissive-Avoidant** people need to work to improve their view of others and learn to trust and rely on them.
- **Anxious-Preoccupied** people need to work to improve their view of themselves and increase their self-reliance.
- **Fearful-Avoidants** need to work to develop an underlying feeling of safety with themselves and others.

Improve your Relationship with Yourself

- Establish individuality: Discover and define your unique needs, desires, values, and beliefs. Express these aspects through your personality and actions, revealing your distinct identity. By aligning your choices with what truly matters to you, you reinforce your individuality and empower yourself to contribute authentically to the world and achieve greater personal fulfillment.

- Limit Expectations - Go with the Flow.
- Practice Self-Compassion: Be kind and compassionate toward yourself, especially during times of difficulty or challenge. Treat yourself with the same warmth and understanding you would offer to a friend in need.
- Engage in hobbies and creative outlets: Make time for activities that bring you joy and fulfillment, such as painting, gardening, playing music, or cooking. Creative expression can be a powerful way to express yourself and relieve stress.
- Practice mindfulness: Engage in mindfulness meditation, deep breathing exercises, or mindful awareness of daily activities to cultivate present-moment awareness and reduce stress.
- Practice gratitude: Cultivate gratitude by reflecting on things you're grateful for daily. Keep a gratitude journal, or take a few moments to appreciate the positive aspects of your life.
- Set realistic goals: Break large tasks or goals into smaller, manageable steps, and celebrate your progress. Focus on what you can control and be gentle with yourself if things don't go as planned.
- See failure as an opportunity to learn: Adjusting your mindset promotes a growth mindset, encourages risk-taking, builds resilience, and fosters innovation and creativity. Over time, reducing your fear of failure can bring a sense of curiosity, adventure, and greater self-efficacy. My philosophy is to fail fast. By adjusting my expectations that there will be bumps in the road when doing something

new, my goal shifts from perfection or avoidance of failure by inaction to getting to the learning lesson quicker so I can adapt and grow.

- Spend time in nature: Connect with the natural world by spending time outdoors, whether walking in the park, hiking in the mountains or simply sitting in your backyard. Nature has a calming and grounding effect on mental health.
- Get adequate sleep: Prioritize restful sleep by establishing a consistent sleep schedule, creating a relaxing bedtime routine, and minimizing screen time before bed. Aim for 7-9 hours of quality sleep each night.
- Limit Media Consumption: Be mindful of the time you spend on news and social media, especially if it causes stress or anxiety. Set boundaries around screen time and prioritize activities that nourish your well-being.

Improve your Relationship with Others (also see the section on Social Self-Care)

- Establish Healthy Boundaries: Set boundaries with others to protect your time, energy, and emotional well-being. Learn to say no when necessary and prioritize activities that nourish and support you.
- Utilize assertive communication: By expressing your needs and boundaries, you can better build healthy relationships with reciprocal energy exchanges. This also improves conflict resolution, builds self-esteem, and allows you to advocate for others better, reducing overall stress.
- Connect with Others: Maintain supportive relationships

with friends, family members, or support groups. Schedule regular check-ins or social activities to foster connection and belonging.

- Limit Exposure to People that Drain Your Energy.
- Express appreciation and gratitude to others: Express appreciation and gratitude for the people in your life by acknowledging their contributions, strengths, and efforts. Small gestures of kindness, recognition, and gratitude can strengthen bonds and enhance the quality of relationships.
- Resolve conflicts constructively: Approach conflicts or disagreements with a willingness to listen, understand, and find mutually satisfactory solutions. Practice active listening, empathy, and compromise to address conflicts constructively and strengthen relationships.
- Be supportive and encouraging: Support, encourage, and validate the people in your life during good times and challenging moments. Show empathy, compassion, and understanding, and lend a listening ear or a helping hand when needed.
- Cultivate shared interests and activities: Engage in shared interests, hobbies, or activities to foster connection and rapport with others. Spending quality time together and creating joyous memories can strengthen bonds and deepen relationships.
- Respect differences: Embrace and celebrate diversity in personalities, perspectives, and experiences among the people in your life. Be open-minded and nonjudgmental, and appreciate each individual's unique qualities that are brought to the relationship.
- Practice forgiveness and acceptance: Cultivate forgiveness, acceptance, and compassion toward yourself and others.

Let go of grudges, resentments, and past hurts, and focus on moving forward with understanding, empathy, and a willingness to repair and rebuild relationships.

- Develop empathy: Practice empathy by actively listening to others, trying to understand their perspectives, and acknowledging their feelings and experiences. Empathy fosters understanding, compassion, and deeper connections in relationships.
- Communicate openly and honestly: Foster open and honest communication by expressing yourself clearly and respectfully, sharing your thoughts, feelings, and needs, and listening attentively to others without judgment or defensiveness. Effective communication builds trust, fosters understanding, and strengthens relationships.
- Build trust: Cultivate trust in your relationships by being reliable, consistent, and accountable in your actions and commitments. Demonstrate integrity, honesty, and respect for others' boundaries to establish a foundation of trust and mutual respect.

Seek Professional Help

Reaching out to a therapist, counselor, or mental health professional for support and guidance is a beautiful way to fast-track progress in understanding yourself and navigating your relationships with others. Therapy can provide a safe and confidential space to explore your thoughts, feelings, and concerns and offers value in many different areas, such as:

- Expertise and specialized knowledge: Mental health professionals have extensive training and expertise in understanding psychological processes, diagnosing mental health disorders, and providing effective treatment interventions. Their specialized knowledge enables them to offer tailored support and evidence-based strategies to address your unique needs and challenges.

- Validation and support: Discussing your thoughts, feelings, and experiences with a mental health professional can provide validation and support. They offer a safe, nonjudgmental space to express yourself openly, feel understood, and receive empathy and validation for your emotions and experiences.

- Access to various treatment options: Mental health professionals can offer various treatment options, including therapy modalities, medication management, and other interventions. They can help you explore different approaches and develop a personalized treatment plan that fits your needs, preferences, and goals.

- Crisis intervention and safety planning: In times of crisis or acute distress, mental health professionals can provide immediate support, crisis intervention, and safety planning. They can help you navigate challenging situations, manage overwhelming emotions, and connect you with additional resources or services to ensure your safety and well-being.

- Skill-building and coping strategies: Mental health professionals can teach you practical skills and coping strategies to manage stress, regulate emotions, challenge negative thought patterns, and improve interpersonal relationships. These skills empower you to cope more effectively with life's challenges and build resilience.

- Early intervention and prevention: Seeking professional help early on can prevent mental health issues from worsening and developing into more severe or chronic conditions. Mental health professionals can identify warning signs, assess risk factors, and intervene early to address underlying issues and prevent future problems.

- A holistic approach to wellness: Mental health professionals take a holistic approach to wellness, considering the interconnectedness of your mental, emotional, physical, and social well-being. They can help you address underlying factors contributing to your mental health concerns and support you in creating a balanced and fulfilling life that promotes overall well-being.

- Progress monitoring and accountability: Working with a mental health professional provides accountability and structure to your self-care journey. They can help you set realistic goals, track progress, and adjust your treatment plan, ensuring you make meaningful strides toward improved mental health and well-being.

Journal Prompts for Mental Health and Well-Being

- How do I currently feel about my mental health and well-being?
- What are my most significant sources of stress or anxiety right now?
- What self-care practices have I found helpful in managing my mental health?
- How do I prioritize my mental well-being in my daily life?

- What are my strengths and coping mechanisms when facing mental health challenges?
- What signs or symptoms indicate that my mental health may be suffering?
- How do I practice self-compassion and self-kindness when I'm struggling mentally?
- What activities or hobbies bring me joy and help me relax?
- How do I set boundaries to protect my mental health and energy?
- What negative thought patterns or beliefs do I notice, and how do they impact my mental well-being?
- How do I seek support from others when I'm struggling with my mental health?
- What habits or behaviors contribute to my mental health and well-being?
- What goals or intentions do I have for improving my mental health?
- How do I cultivate gratitude and mindfulness to promote mental well-being?
- What role do physical activity and exercise play in supporting my mental well-being?
- How do I navigate challenges or setbacks in my mental health journey with resilience and perseverance?
- What strategies do I use to manage overwhelming emotions or intrusive thoughts?
- How do I foster meaningful connections and social support to boost my mental well-being?
- How do I feel about working with a professional to support/improve my mental health?
- How do I celebrate my progress and achievements in prioritizing my mental health and well-being?

5

EMOTIONAL SELF-CARE

"Self-care is giving yourself permission to pause." -
Cecilia Tran

E motional intelligence (EI) effectively recognizes, understands, manages, expresses, and modulates emotions. It requires a set of skills and competencies that can be learned and improved upon to navigate social interactions, communicate more effectively, and make informed decisions based on emotional cues. Our feelings and emotions are signals that speak an internal language, and EI aims to tap into that language and speak it more effectively. If you've ever had a "gut feeling" or "intuition" that something felt unsafe and you altered your behavior based on that feeling, that is emotional intelligence at work. This dynamic plays out in all areas of life, not just situations where our safety is threatened. It just takes some refinement and tuning to listen to those messages when they aren't as "loud." EI is also the skill that allows us to pause to consider information and emotions before responding to others. It allows us to engage maturely and manage our relationships with more compassion.

Identifying Emotions

The first step to becoming emotionally intelligent is recognizing and naming your emotions as they arise within you. Once we can identify them in ourselves, we can recognize them in others more easily. There are many ways to build your skills in this area, but building your emotional vocabulary is a great starting point.

There are a variety of visual tools that can help to bolster one's skill in recognizing emotions. The "Emotional Guidance Scale" allows individuals to become more aware of current emotional states. It provides a framework to identify and label emotions and then further classify those emotions on a continuum from positive to negative. The scale also gives a framework for the intentional choices about thoughts and actions necessary to move up the emotional scale. By practicing pausing and experiencing the emotion instead of reacting to it, we can cultivate a belief that emotion is a personal choice. We can not choose what happens in the outside world or how others may treat us, but we can control how we respond. According to Abraham Hicks, the following continuum of emotions make up the emotional scale:

- Joy/Appreciation/Empowerment/Freedom/Love
- Passion
- Enthusiasm/Eagerness/Happiness
- Positive Expectation/Belief

- Optimism
- Hopefulness
- Contentment
- Boredom
- Pessimism
- Frustration/Irritation/Impatience
- Overwhelmed (feeling overwhelmed)
- Disappointment
- Doubt
- Worry
- Blame
- Discouragement
- Anger
- Revenge
- Hatred/Rage
- Jealousy
- Insecurity/Guilt/Unworthiness
- Fear/Grief/Desperation/Despair/Powerlessness

Converting the Emotional Scale into an "Emotion Spiral" diagram can be a helpful tool. For some, the linear representation of the scale makes perfect sense. However, visual learners might find added value in conceptualizing the list as two spirals of emotion. The organic twisting of upward and downward spirals reflects how we often talk about emotions in everyday life.

We've all experienced days where negative events seem to stack up, making us expect the rest of the day to unfold in the same way. This confirmation bias creates a self-fulfilling prophecy, where we look for evidence to support feelings of bad luck or that others are working against us.

Using the "Emotion Spiral" tool helps visualize how giving negative emotions more energy, thought, and attention can pull us further down the spiral. By pausing and choosing non-reaction, we can shift our awareness. Pairing this pause with self-care tools from this book allows us to move into an upward spiral of emotions.

Asking yourself, "What would it take to get to the next positive emotion above where I'm at right now?" is a powerful way to practice pausing and actively seek better feelings. Another effective way to use the Emotional Guidance Chart or Emotion Spiral is to check your emotions at multiple points in the day. For example, identify what you're feeling in the morning, then check back in during the afternoon or evening. This process can provide 2-3 data points to track whether you're spiraling upward, downward, or staying relatively fixed in your emotional state.

UPWARD SPIRAL   DOWNWARD SPIRAL

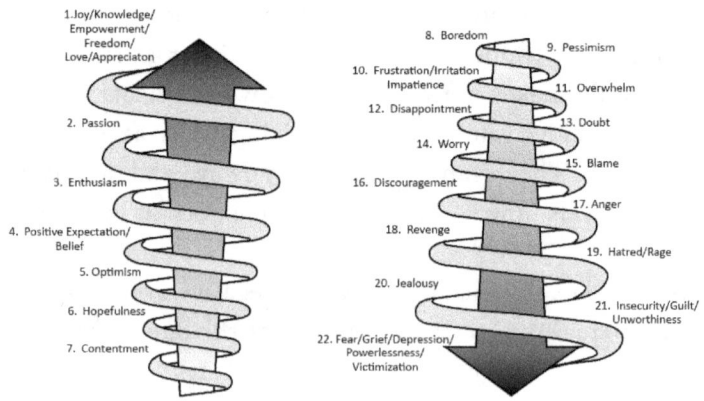

Emotion wheels are another tool to categorize emotions. Wheels organize emotions into primary, secondary, and tertiary categories, visually representing the range of human emotions. They can help identify core human emotions, and the more nuanced relationship emotions have with each other. Emotion wheels help expand our emotional vocabulary, giving us a framework to consider how slight variations in emotion feel within our body when we're feeling delight versus satisfaction. They are very similar and fall within the "joy" core emotion. Still, delight is a stronger feeling of joy sparked by unexpected, extraordinary, or delightful experiences. In contrast, satisfaction is a feeling of contentment and fulfillment, often when one's expectations, desires, or needs are met or exceeded. It brings about a sense of relief or comfort.

One of the earlier emotion wheels designed by William James listed only four core emotions at the center of the wheel: Fear, Grief, Love, and Rage. I prefer the Junto Institute's expanded Emotion Wheel, built from an expanded core emotion base of six feelings: Love, Joy, Surprise, Sadness, Anger, and Fear. The core emotions are typically easier to identify. As you become more adept at identifying your emotions, you will be able to recognize more of the secondary and tertiary emotions that relate to the core emotions and branch out from the center of the wheel. One great exercise is to pick an emotion on the secondary or tertiary portion of the wheel and seek to experience that emotion during the week. Create experiences that might trigger that response within you and notice what it feels like in your body.

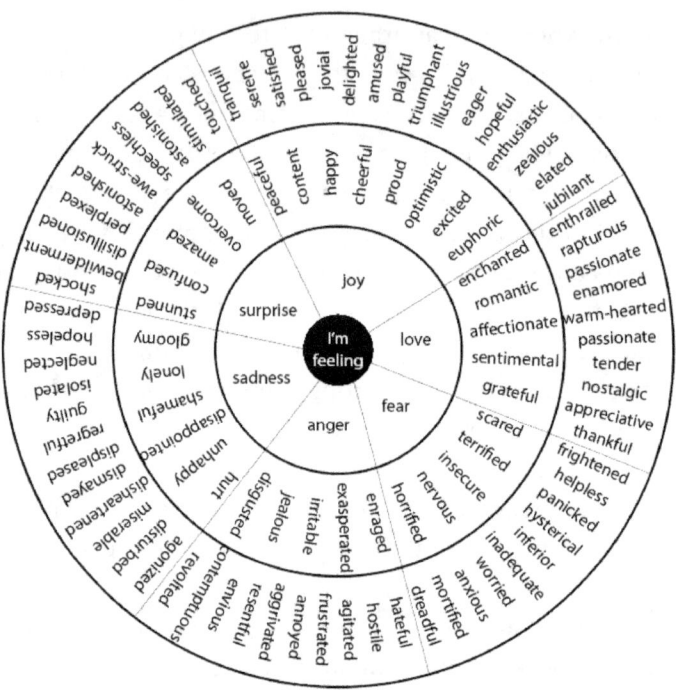

Recreated from the Junto Institute's Emotion Wheel

Building Self-Awareness

Self-awareness is essential in building emotional intelligence. By accurately identifying the range of emotions and tying them to present-moment experiences, we create an opportunity to learn and grow from that information. This can be achieved through 4 primary methodologies:

1. Self-Reflection: Taking the time to turn inward and analyze your thoughts and feelings. Meditation, jour-

naling, or quiet contemplation can help you recognize your emotions.

2. Body Awareness: Pay attention to the physical sensations that arise with particular emotional states. Changes in heart rate, breathing rate, muscle tension, or even our coping strategies, like how we hold our body, cross our legs or arms, touch our face, or hold our gaze, all provide cues that can help identify emotions in the future.

3. Contextual Analysis: Reflecting on the circumstances surrounding a situation or event that triggers a particular emotional state can also provide helpful information over time. This can help us better understand the self-care necessary to soothe and protect our emotional state when we encounter similar situations in the future. Situations that proceed with an emotional trigger or heightened emotional response provide great information.

4. Seek Feedback from Others: Asking trusted friends, family members, or mental health professionals for their perspectives on your emotional state can be incredibly valuable. We all have blind spots to the consistency with which we unconsciously react to specific triggers. Requesting this feedback from the safety of a calm and neutral space can better prepare us to self-reflect and observe when we are experiencing that trigger in real-time.

Here are some ideas to explore to build self-awareness around emotional triggers and your emotional states.

1. Print copies of whichever emotional tool resonates with you best (emotional scale, wheel, chart, or spiral). Keep

copies where you spend the most time: in your office, your car's visor or console, your wallet or purse, tucked into a journal or attached to your fridge. The key is to keep the reference tool handy to access it whenever you're experiencing an emotion you're struggling to identify. Refer to the reference tool and name the emotion while experiencing it. You can also use these tools as conversation starters with friends, family members, or coworkers to facilitate conversations about feelings or experiences.

2. Play games to track emotions. You can use tick marks next to emotions to see how many times you feel certain emotions in a day, week, or month. This helps build a valuable data set to recognize patterns over time. Recognizing patterns and emotions more quickly makes identifying more nuanced differences between feelings easier.

3. Emotion Journaling is a highly beneficial tool. Regularly write down your emotions and experiences and reference the emotional guidance scale, spiral, or wheel. You can free-form and reference the tools for daily "diary-style" entries or write a single emotion at the top of each 2-page spread. Over a week or month, list the situation, experience, or person that triggered those emotions so you can begin to see consistencies in your experience. This is an exceptional way to identify toxic situations, environments, and people you may want to reconsider giving access to your time and energy.

4. Emotional Charades is a great game to explore. It is fun to role-play with trusted friends and families and act out different emotions without speaking. Move your face and body in various ways to communicate certain emotions

and see if participants can guess. This silly game is usually quite fun and a great way to deepen your connections with others by getting feedback on your ability to connect expression to emotional states that others recognize.

5. Use mantras or affirmations to help bring awareness to emotional states and build belief systems that help regulate emotions. Write out any sample mantras listed below on sticky notes and post them throughout your home, car, and office to remind yourself to prioritize emotional self-care.

- "How does this make me feel?"
- "I seek to understand before I react."
- "Discomfort is an opportunity for growth."
- "I choose to respond, not react."
- "Even this shall pass."
- "I am resilient in navigating life's challenges."
- "I am aware of my emotions but not defined by them."
- "I give my emotions space to be seen, heard, and known."

If you want to take further stock of your Emotional Intelligence, there are assessments available online:

- Emotional Intelligence 2.0 Assessment
- EQ-i 2.0 Emotional Intelligence Assessment
- Mayer-Salovey-Caruso Emotional Intelligence Test (MS-CEIT)

Pattern Recognition

As you progress in your ability to identify and name your emotions, you can begin to notice any patterns that develop from the data you've compiled by making note of your triggers and the frequency or absence of certain emotions from your experience. This is a crucial step in building emotional intelligence by shedding light on unconscious beliefs and patterning or identifying the meaning we've attached to specific experiences (our stories). Our social conditioning, cultural influences, or past traumas can often create an unspoken "rule" that we follow to feel safe in our environment even long after the climate has changed. Challenging those rules and learning ways of experiencing the world gives us more opportunities to create the life we want. Bringing your journal or data to a therapist is a beneficial tool to create a starting point to break old patterns and get personalized ideas to create change in your life.

- Analyze your data
- Analyze the data in the journal you've been using or the tick marks you've made on the emotional charts/wheels/scales.
- Are there certain emotions you experience more quickly or frequently than others?
- Are there certain emotions absent from your experience?
- Reflect on your answers to the above questions—Journal about it.
- Continue to monitor, identify, and track your feelings and see if you can start to experience the more nuanced emotions in the outer rings of the emotion wheel.
- Reflect on your family dynamics, personality traits, cultural influences, social environment, and past traumas to see if you can identify why some situations easily trigger you and why some emotions rarely show up in your experience. This can be an excellent starting point for

working with a therapist or coach to explore and expand your emotional horizons. As an example, unless it was modeled in the family unit, it is typical for women to quickly experience anger by filtering it into hurt and for men to filter sadness into anger. In extreme cases, like my own, it has taken a decade to recognize and name anger within my body. Cultural and gender norms are passed down through generations about how we, as women and men, "should" behave. Unless we consciously challenge those norms, they will continue to limit the richness and full range of human experience.

Self-Regulation

The moment of real EI transformation comes when you feel an intense emotion rising within your body and consciously pause before responding. Only some comments, emails, or conversations require your immediate response. This simple act of owning your time can lead to tremendous growth in feelings of self-worth and confidence. You deserve the time you need to put your best self forward. Impulsivity can often lead to regret. Thoughtful communication is typically more aligned with our value system.

Practicing statements that give you the time you need to process is perfectly acceptable. Practice saying things like:

- "I hear what you're saying. I want time to consider what you've said before responding."
- "I appreciate your response. I'll respond shortly".
- "Hmm.Interesting. Give me some time to think about that."

You don't owe anyone the immediacy of your time. Take care

of yourself and practice the pause. This allows you to reflect, process, and consider where you might be attaching meaning from previous experiences and automatically applying them to this situation. When you take the time to attend to the physical manifestations within your body that arise with that triggered emotion, you are conducting both emotional, mental, and physical self-care and being more mindful of your response, which is also excellent social self-care. If it's a coworker, it's also excellent professional self-care. It is all connected. By taking care of yourself, you take care of your relationships and the wholeness of your life.

We all have different ways that we've learned to cope with challenging emotions. We all have a baseline set of tools when processing difficult emotions. Some people go for a run. Some call their best friend to vent or contact their therapist for support. Others may turn to food, alcohol, drugs, social media, or binge-watch TV to numb out and avoid feeling that emotion entirely. Take time to consider your go-to coping mechanisms and take stock of which support your general self-care and which do not. If you know you tend to numb out, can you commit to doing something else for one week to experience your world differently? Perhaps you go for a short walk around the block or close yourself in your bedroom to punch your bed pillow when you feel angry to dissipate that energy before you say anything you'd regret to your loved ones. Or maybe when you're sad, you commit to laying on a foam roller lengthwise to open up your heart space and let the emotion pass. If tears come, let them. The quickest way through an emotion is to experience it fully. And the fastest way to make that happen is by attending to our nervous system to help regulate it. Go back to Chapter 2 and experiment with any of the tools for nervous system regulation. Deep breathing, mindfulness meditation, progressive muscle relaxation, or other techniques listed in that section will give you the calmness and grounding to craft a more thoughtful response or mindfully reengage with others. Repeat the process if you get relaxed and get triggered again while trying to respond. It is good training to modulate back and forth from a calm state to practice the process. It's perfectly acceptable to take more time.

Emotional Expression

Once you understand the range of emotions and what you experience daily, you can begin to develop the external communication of those emotions. Expressing your feelings authentically and constructively, verbally and nonverbally, through assertive and empathetic conversation helps you build trust and rapport with others. This skill is the basis of real vulnerability and intimacy with others and is critical in forming meaningful relationships that nurture your soul.

- Active Listening: Active listening requires being fully present and engaged with what someone is saying. Suspend your desire to interject with your experience of the same situation or share your thoughts/opinions/judgm ents on what is being shared. Active listening aims to understand what another person is experiencing, identify their emotional experience, and validate those feelings with empathy.
- Use Expressive Language: Use descriptive language to express your emotions and paint a picture of your experience for someone. You can ask your listener to withhold their thoughts, feelings, impressions, opinions, etc., until you

are done or specifically ask for the type of response you're looking for.

- Use Metaphors and Analogies: Metaphors and analogies can help describe emotions in a way that is more accessible, relatable, and understandable.
- Share your experiences: Using personal anecdotes and experiences related to an emotion discussed can help convey empathy and understanding. Recognizing yourself in another's experience and vice versa can help build connections between people and dissolve feelings of loneliness. The simple act of being seen and known within our emotional experience is very liberating.
- Non-Verbal Cues: Recognize that verbal communication is only part of emotional expression. Our faces and body language express a whole story on their own. Ensure your face/body communication aligns with your verbal statements. This helps the words you share carry more weight.

Emotionally Intelligent Decision-Making

You can live more intentionally by building more time and space between the emotional trigger and how you respond to the emotions that arise. Slowing things down allows you to tap into your intuition and honor the things that are important to you. When you consider why you're triggered and can unpack the stories and conditioning that may be playing into your initial gut reaction, you can take greater responsibility for your emotional health and well-being. Leaning into the pause frees up much energy to choose words that align with your value system and logic, creating a more well-rounded response. This builds confidence over time. When you can assertively communicate your feelings without falling victim to your immediate emotions, you'll feel a sense of pride in that accomplishment, and the stress/overwhelm of emotional triggers begins to lose power over you. When you have a system to manage emotions and realize you can't control other people but CAN control your responses to them, you gain control over your life.

Be patient with yourself as you're learning this new skill. It can be challenging to break old patterns, so give yourself grace and commit to doing your best every day. If you would like additional support around developing this skill, hiring a licensed therapist can help you cover a lot of ground much quicker. By writing down emotional triggers and talking them over with your therapist weekly before responding, you can permit yourself to consider things and have a partner to hold you accountable to take the actions you decide will best support your health. You can also get exposed to other modalities like cognitive-behavioral therapy (CBT) and dialectical behavior therapy (DBT), which can help individuals explore and understand their emotions in a supportive and guided environment. Therapists can provide insights, tools, and techniques for managing emotions effectively.

Journal Prompts for Emotional Health and Well-Being

- What emotions am I experiencing right now, and what triggered them?
- How do I typically respond to strong emotions, such as anger, sadness, or anxiety?
- What are my core emotional needs, and how do I meet them?

- How do I recognize and label my emotions accurately?
- What physical sensations do I notice when experiencing different emotions?
- What are my go-to strategies for regulating my emotions when I feel overwhelmed?
- How do I express emotions and communicate needs to others?
- What patterns have I noticed in my emotional experiences?
- What beliefs or assumptions do I hold about emotions, and how do they influence my behavior?
- How do I practice self-compassion and kindness towards myself when struggling emotionally?
- What coping mechanisms or self-soothing techniques do I find most effective?
- How do my emotions impact my relationships and interactions with others?
- What unresolved emotional wounds or traumas do I carry, and how do they affect me today?
- How do I cultivate resilience and bounce back from setbacks?
- What activities or practices help me connect with and healthily process my emotions?
- How do I distinguish between my emotions and those of others, especially regarding empathy and boundary-setting?
- What are my triggers for specific emotional reactions, and how can I manage them more effectively?
- How do I foster emotional intelligence in my daily life, personally and professionally?
- What role does mindfulness play in my emotional awareness and regulation?

- How do I envision my emotional growth and development in the future?

6

SOCIAL SELF-CARE

"When we fulfill our own needs first, we become a wellspring of love and compassion for others." - Deepak Chopra

Social self-care encompasses activities and practices that nurture and support our social connections, relationships, and sense of belonging. It involves prioritizing meaningful interactions, cultivating supportive networks, and engaging in activities that promote connection and community. Social self-care is essential for maintaining emotional well-being, reducing loneliness and isolation, and fostering a sense of belonging and connection to others. Investing in social health can enhance our overall quality of life and build resilience during life's challenges.

The 5 Levels of Intimacy

Understanding the five levels of intimacy is a powerful framework for social self-care because it allows individuals to assess the depth and quality of their relationships and ensure they invest time and energy into connections that provide the support and fulfillment they need. By cultivating relationships at more profound levels of intimacy, individuals can experience greater emotional connection, validation, and empathy, leading to improved well-being and resilience in the face of life's challenges. Also, having relationships spanning multiple levels of intimacy can provide a well-rounded support network that meets various social and emotional needs. Take stock of the relationships you have in your life, from co-workers, acquaintances, friends, family, and partners. A well-rounded assortment of relationships that fall into these categories can create a sense of belonging and connection.

1. **Safe Communication or Surface Communication:** At level 1, interactions are superficial and revolve around small talk, casual topics, and general information sharing. Surface communication may include discussing the weather, sharing basic personal details, or engaging in polite conversation in social settings. While this level of interaction is necessary for initiating connections, it typically lacks depth and emotional intimacy.

2. **Facts, Opinions, and Beliefs:** At level 2, individuals share more personal information, including opinions, preferences, and factual details about their lives. Conversations may delve into hobbies, interests, work, and current events. While still relatively superficial, this level of intimacy involves some degree of self-disclosure and can help individuals find common ground and build rapport.

3. **Thoughts and Feelings:** At level 3, individuals begin

to take risks by sharing their thoughts, feelings, and emotions more openly and authentically. Conversations become more meaningful and vulnerable as people express their hopes, fears, dreams, and concerns. Sharing personal experiences, struggles, and successes deepens the emotional connection between individuals and fosters empathy, understanding, and support. At this stage, information shared must be received without judgment or criticism, or the relationship will not continue to deepen over time.

4. **Needs and Desires:** Level 4 involves sharing deeper desires, needs, and values central to one's identity and well-being. Individuals express their core beliefs, aspirations, and vulnerabilities, seeking validation, acceptance, and support from others. Discussions may center around personal goals, greatest joys, previous mistakes, fears of rejection, or desires for intimacy and connection. Building relationships at this level requires trust, empathy, mutual respect, and a great deal of vulnerability because we can't change the details of our past choices or experiences. We must trust that we will be accepted for the wholeness of who we are and that our previous mistakes, poor judgment, or lack of integrity will not define who we are in the present moment. We trust that we will be seen for who we are today and that our past is simply part of our journey to this moment.

5. **Core Identity:** The fifth and highest level of intimacy involves sharing one's core identity, including deeply held beliefs, values, traumas, and insecurities. At this level, individuals reveal their true selves authentically and without reservation, allowing others to completely accept

and understand them. Intimate relationships at this level are characterized by unconditional love, trust, and emotional safety. This level requires the most significant amount of trust and vulnerability.

Relationship Assessment Tests

Interpersonal and relational assessment tests are crucial components of a self-care plan for social health as they provide valuable insights into individual communication styles, relationship dynamics, and emotional needs. By understanding these factors, individuals can develop a deeper awareness of themselves and their interactions with others, leading to more fulfilling and supportive relationships. These assessments help individuals identify areas for improvement, establish healthy boundaries, and develop effective communication and conflict-resolution skills, all essential for maintaining positive social connections and overall well-being. Incorporating interpersonal and relational assessment tests into a self-care plan empowers individuals to nurture their social health, prioritize meaningful relationships, and cultivate a supportive network that contributes to their happiness and resilience.

- **The Relationship Assessment Scale (RAS)**: This scale measures relationship satisfaction across several dimensions, including communication, conflict resolution, intimacy, and overall happiness.
- **The Gottman Relationship Checkup**: Developed by Drs. John and Julie Gottman, this assessment tool evaluates a relationship's strengths and challenges based on the Gottman Method, which focuses on communication, conflict resolution, friendship, and shared meaning.

- **The Five Love Languages**: Based on the book by Dr. Gary Chapman, this assessment identifies individuals' primary love languages—words of affirmation, acts of service, receiving gifts, quality time, and physical touch—to help couples understand and meet each other's emotional needs.

- **The Interpersonal Communication Inventory (ICI)**: This assessment evaluates communication patterns and relationship styles, including listening skills, assertiveness, conflict management, and nonverbal communication.

- **The Conflict Resolution Styles Inventory**: This inventory assesses individuals' preferred approaches to resolving conflicts within relationships, such as collaboration, compromise, avoidance, accommodation, or competition.

- **The Attachment Style Questionnaire**: This assessment explores individuals' attachment styles—secure, anxious-preoccupied, dismissive-avoidant, or fearful-avoidant—and how they impact relationship dynamics, intimacy, and emotional connection.

- **The Personal Assessment of Intimacy in Relationships (PAIR)**: Developed by Dr. Mark H. Davis, this assessment evaluates intimacy levels in relationships across various dimensions, including emotional, social, sexual, and intellectual intimacy.

- **The Relationship Dynamics Scale (RDS):** This scale measures relationship dynamics and satisfaction across multiple dimensions, including communication, trust, commitment, and conflict resolution.

Deepen the Connections You Already Have

It is well documented through scientific research that loneliness is a risk factor for many health issues and that social connection serves as a protective shield against stress. According to the World Health Organization (WHO) and the Centers for Disease Control (CDC), social isolation is a serious public health issue linked to issues like smoking, obesity, and sedentary lifestyles, as well as a 50% increase in dementia, 29% increase in heart disease, 32% increase in stroke, and significant ties to increased anxiety, depression, and suicide. There is something innate in our human conditioning that wires us for social interaction, and failing to invest time and energy into this vital aspect of life can have severe consequences for our overall health and well-being. Here are some ideas to deepen the connections you already have.

1) Cultivate intimacy:

- Share something vulnerable.
- Prepare a favorite meal or plan a surprise outing together.
- Hug your friends regularly or share other forms of physical affection.
- Do something silly, like leaving a cute note on their car or making a secret handshake.
- Prioritize quality time - remain present and focused while spending time together. Put your phones away.
- Practice active listening. Paraphrase what your friends are telling you to be sure you understand.
- Use your friend/family member's name repeatedly - research has shown it deepens connection.
- Express gratitude and appreciation. A heartfelt "thank you," whether verbal or in writing, can strengthen a connection.

- Cultivate shared experiences and interests - Take the initiative to hang out and commit to consistent communication.

2) Create rituals and traditions:

- Celebrate birthdays, holidays, anniversaries.
- Have a weekly or monthly movie, puzzle, or game night.
- Create seasonal experiences to anticipate together (e.g., sitting around the fire pit, BBQing, camping).
- Celebrate successes and milestones:

1. Take your friend out to dinner to celebrate a promotion.
2. You can drop off a housewarming gift to friends who buy a new home or offer to come over for a demo or painting party to help them make the house their home.
3. Throw a surprise baby shower or birthday party.

3) Support each other's growth:

- Check in on others' progress toward goals.
- Discuss forming an agreement around being accountability partners.
- Order food that doesn't tempt a friend to get off track, respecting their boundaries regarding dietary restrictions or weight loss plans.

Make New Adult Friends

While it may seem daunting initially, making new friends can be surprisingly easy with an open mind, a willingness to step out of our comfort zones, and a genuine interest in getting to know others. By initiating conversations, attending social events, joining clubs or groups, and being open to new experiences, we can create meaningful connections and cultivate rewarding friendships that enrich our lives in countless ways. Set a goal to make one new friend this month. Explore the list below or develop your ideas to meet new people or leverage the networks you already have to actively find someone you'd like to get to know better as a friend.

1) Meet Complete Strangers (Yikes!):

- Pursue Your Interests: Engage in activities or hobbies you enjoy. Whether joining a sports league, taking a cooking class, or attending a book club, shared interests provide a natural way to connect with others. By carving out time to do something you already love to do but doing it in a group setting, you increase the likelihood of connecting with others who have shared passions.
- Volunteer: Volunteering for a cause you care about is a great way to meet like-minded people and give back to the community.
- Attend Meetups and Social Events: Use platforms like Meetup.com to find events and groups in your area that align with your interests. Meet new people at social gatherings, networking events, or community activities by setting a goal to introduce yourself to at least three people.
- Take a Class or Workshop: Enroll in a class or workshop to learn something new. This can be a great way to meet people with similar interests while gaining new skills.
- Join a Club or Organization: Look for local clubs or organizations that align with your interests, such as a hiking group, a photography club, or a gaming community.

THE ULTIMATE SELF-CARE HANDBOOK

- Use social media and Online Platforms: Join online communities or groups related to your interests. While these connections are virtual, they can lead to real-life friendships.
- Network at Work or Professional Events: Engage with colleagues and attend work-related social events. This can help you form connections with people you work with.
- Attend Religious or Spiritual Gatherings: If you're religious or spiritual, attending services or joining related groups can be a way to meet people with similar beliefs.

2) Close the Gaps:

- Reach out to friends of friends or let your current friends know you're looking to expand your circle of friends. More than likely, your current friends know "the perfect person" they'd like to set you up with for a friendship.
- Convert a co-worker into a friend: This can be tricky if you're highly mindful or concerned about professional boundaries or leading a team. However, it can be an excellent way to expand your existing circle of friends by selectively connecting with co-workers outside the professional setting. It can start as a mutual friendship to work toward professional career goals, holding each other accountable to a professional development plan, or a joint commitment to a personal weight loss/exercise plan. Joint goals can often lead to the frequency of contact and low-pressure situations where friendships can naturally unfold.
- Befriend someone you consistently see working out at the gym or who attends group fitness classes with you. You

already share common interests and goals. It's an easy transition to approach someone you see consistently to start saying hi, using their name, and talking about their fitness goals. Over time, you may find other interests that could lead to connecting outside that environment.

- Reconnect with Old Friends: Reach out to old friends or acquaintances. Reconnecting with someone you already know can be a way to expand your social circle.

3) Adjust your Behavior and Expectations:

- Be Open and Approachable: Smile, make eye contact, and be willing to initiate conversations. Being approachable makes it easier for others to engage with you.
- Be Consistent: Regular attendance increases your chances of forming connections. Consistently attend events or activities with a higher likelihood of attendees having shared interests.
- Invite People to Do Things: Take the initiative to invite people to coffee, lunch, or an event. This shows that you're interested in building a friendship.
- Be Patient: Building new friendships takes time. Be patient and allow relationships to develop naturally.
- Make the first move: Like in dating, someone must acknowledge that you enjoy each other's company and want to deepen the connection. Challenge yourself to be courageous. You might be one sentence away from having more friends!

Journal Prompts for Social Health and Well-Being

- What role do relationships play in my life, and how do they contribute to my well-being?
- Who are the most important people in my life, and why are they significant to me?
- What qualities do I value most in my relationships with others?
- How do I communicate my needs, boundaries, and expectations in my relationships?
- What patterns or dynamics do I notice in my interactions with others, both positive and negative?
- What are my strengths and areas for growth in building and maintaining relationships?
- How do I nurture and cultivate meaningful connections with family, friends, and colleagues?
- What conflicts or challenges have I encountered in my relationships, and how have I navigated them?
- How do I show appreciation and express love to the people in my life?
- What role do empathy and compassion play in my interactions with others?
- How do I prioritize quality time and connection in my relationships amidst a busy schedule?
- What boundaries do I need to set to protect my well-being in my relationships?
- How do I handle criticism or feedback from others, and how do I respond constructively?
- What role does forgiveness play in my relationships, and how do I practice forgiveness?
- How do I balance my social life, personal goals, and aspirations?
- What new social connections do I want to cultivate?

- How do I navigate changes or transitions in my social circle or relationships?
- How do I support the growth and development of the people I care about?
- What are my values and beliefs about friendship, love, and community?
- How do I contribute positively to the well-being and happiness of the people in my life?

7

PROFESSIONAL SELF-CARE

"Never get so busy making a living that you forget to make a life."
- Dolly Parton

Self-care within the workplace is an essential component in overall health and well-being. Seeking meaningful work opportunities in businesses with a supportive and positive culture can help foster an environment where self-care and work-life balance are valued. Toxic or high-stress workplace cultures often undermine self-care by promoting overwork, disregard for personal boundaries, and stigmatizing employees who don't abide by the company values. Ironically, these high-stress environments are precisely where self-care is most needed. We are paying attention to how we feel and how our attempts to advocate and promote our sense of well-being at the office can shed much light on whether the company or role is a good fit for you. Ideally, we strive to find work that aligns with our values, gives us a sense of purpose, and allows for a sense of contribution or impact to the community or society through that company's efforts or products. Part of professional self-care is recognizing when a work environment is not a good match so we can seek alternatives to design a life closer to what we desire. Once we land in a position/company where it is a good fit, ongoing professional self-care seeks to maintain a healthy balance between professional responsibilities and personal life, avoiding overwork and burnout.

Professional Assessments

Professional assessment tests can provide valuable insights into your strengths, weaknesses, and areas for growth, helping you make informed decisions about your career, education, or personal development. These tests offer objective data and feedback that can validate your skills and talents, identify areas for improvement, and guide you toward career paths or opportunities that align with your interests and abilities. By leveraging the results of professional assessment tests, you can gain clarity, confidence, and direction in pursuing your goals and aspirations, ultimately leading to greater fulfillment and success in your endeavors. Here are a few tests that you can take to explore this further.

1. Holland Code Career Test
2. Skills Profiler (U.S. Department of Labor)
3. CliftonStrengths Assessment (formerly StrengthsFinder)
4. 16 Personalities Career Test
5. DISC

Passive Job Seeking

Passive job seeking can be a strategic approach for exploring career opportunities while remaining employed.

- Keep your resume current to act quickly when opportunities present themselves.
- Arrange for automated email alerts for your dream job title whenever positions become available.
- Research your current role to determine the market pay rate for your role/industry. Understand the landscape of value and honestly assess how you fall into it. If you're underpaid, speak up.
- Keep your LinkedIn profile up to date.
- Network consistently.
- Engage with recruiters.
- Follow industry influencers and regularly browse job boards.
- Seek out referrals.

Professional Development

Professional development is essential for advancing your career, acquiring new skills, and staying competitive in today's job market.

- Attend networking events (even if you're an introvert!).
- Attend professional workshops, trainings, seminars, and conferences to engage in continuous learning.
- Stay current with industry trends.
- Spearhead lunchtime TED Talk series to inspire team development.
- Spend one-hour researching side hustle opportunities that could continue to hone your skills, provide additional

income, and build your resume.
- Seek mentors in your field who can offer support and guidance to help you navigate your career path.
- Develop soft skills, including communication, leadership, problem-solving, and emotional intelligence.
- Seek feedback from superiors, peers, and any team members you manage. Improvement can only come from a clearly defined path.
- Keep up-to-date on project management tools to organize your workload and make more room for on-the-job development time.

Boundary Setting

Setting boundaries involves establishing clear expectations and limits around your time, energy, and availability in the workplace. By setting boundaries effectively, you can protect your time, prevent burnout, and maintain a sense of autonomy and control over your workload. While company culture can impact your ability to do this, ultimately, it is our responsibility to uphold our boundaries or seek out other employment with a company with a more aligned culture.

- Set realistic expectations for yourself and others with workload and delivery timelines.
- Prioritize tasks based on urgency and importance and say no to tasks outside the scope of your role.
- Hold boundaries around regular break intervals and take them!
- Establish clear work hours and boundaries for your availability to your employer.
- Understand your state's laws around using personal

phones/computers for work use.
- Set boundaries around your limitations of time and delegate tasks to others.
- Limit interruptions and distractions at work. Discuss "office hours" with your team and set expectations for cell phone use. Also, turn off social media notifications at work.
- Time block and set boundaries around productivity.

Work-Life Balance

Work-life balance is the equilibrium between the time and energy spent on work-related activities and personal pursuits, including family, leisure, and self-care. Achieving work-life balance involves prioritizing and allocating time and resources to various aspects of life to promote overall well-being and fulfillment.

- Take advantage of employee perks and benefits.
- Put your health first and use your sick days to get well.
- Use your vacation time yearly to prevent burnout and recharge your soul.
- Encourage chronic overworkers to go home. As a leader or boss, set an example of work-life balance.
- Check if your employer offers an Employee Assistance Program (EAP) and take advantage of the benefit to screen for your health and well-being.
- If you manage a team, offer a flexible schedule or relaxed dress days.
- Host a team spirit day with costumes, cornhole, or other games.
- Reserve overtime for the occasional big push on a project.

Please don't make it a habit to arrive early and leave late.
- Take a deep breath at the doorstep of your home before you walk in the door. Leave work stressors at work so you can truly enjoy your family.
- Advocate for flexibility in scheduling or arrange for telecommuting, flex hours, or compressed workweeks to create more work-life balance.
- Hire a professional coach if you need support in creating a better work-life balance.

Time Management/Organization

- Take regular breaks throughout your workday.
- Take breaks outside to take in fresh air and sunlight.
- Schedule back-to-back meetings when possible to avoid gaps in unproductive time.
- Use to-do lists or online project management tools to track your priorities and your team's.
- Calendar essential deadlines and milestones.
- Batch similar tasks to increase productivity.
- Avoid multitasking, as it has been linked to decreased productivity.
- Use note-taking tools to capture inspired ideas to reevaluate later.
- Explore different time management techniques such as the Pomodoro Technique, Eisenhower Matrix, or time-blocking.
- Allow time to integrate information to ensure you capture learning lessons.
- Break projects into smaller tasks so projects feel more manageable.

- Take time to review your work and adjust as needed before handoff.

Proactive/Assertive Communication

- Negotiate for a raise. If you are paid less than the national average of 3% annually, it's time to advocate for yourself.
- Ask for clarity about the benefits your employer provides.
- Speak up in meetings.
- Ask your supervisor to help you set up an action plan to get a promotion.
- Contact your supervisor if you're having trouble setting boundaries around time management or have accepted an unrealistic workload that is impacting your ability to set consistent work hours.
- Reinforce boundaries that have been set. Everyone needs reminders sometimes.
- Give people the benefit of the doubt and discuss issues openly.
- Celebrate your successes and those of others.
- Provide feedback to your team or supervisor regarding process improvements, issues needing resolution, etc.
- Make requests of other departments to ease cross-department collaborations and dependencies.
- Advocate for resources to support the successful completion of projects.
- Address microaggressions and inappropriate behavior.
- Clarify expectations on a project to ensure you fully understand what is needed.

Environmental Self-Care in the Workplace

- Decorate/personalize your office, cubicle, or desk. Make it a happy place.
- Keep a list of inspiring words, images, quotes, or affirmations nearby.
- Keep your workstation clean/organized.
- Regularly purge papers and files if applicable.
- Bring a few plants into your workspace to keep the airspace clean.
- Bring an air purifier, diffuser, or small heater (if allowed) to control your personal space better.
- Keep your digital or paper filing system in order.

Physical/Mental/Emotional Self-Care in the Workplace

- Drink water regularly.
- Practice good eye screen health with the 20-20-20 rule. Look 20 feet away from your screen for at least 20 seconds every 20 minutes.
- Take time to connect with co-workers.
- Ensure my workstation is ergonomic and comfortable.
- Stand up and stretch for 5 minutes while composing your response to a challenging email/DM.
- Keep healthy, shelf-stable snacks on your desk.
- Consider a standing desk or pad to change up your current ergonomics.
- Make your lunch an actual break from getting work done. It's the law, and it's there for a reason.
- Consider biking to work.
- Work on your posture.
- Monitor your steps with a fitness tracker. Set challenges with co-workers and aim to lap around the office every

hour.
- Consider a walking meeting. Get outside the office, move your body, improve your blood flow, and see how creative you can be in problem-solving.
- Host a potluck or chili cookoff.

Journal Prompts for Professional Health and Well-Being

- What are my current career goals, both short-term and long-term?
- How do I feel about my current job or career path?
- What strengths and skills do I bring to my professional role?
- What aspects of my job or career do I find most fulfilling?
- What challenges or obstacles do I face professionally, and how do I overcome them?
- What values and principles guide my professional decisions and actions?
- How do I prioritize work-life balance and well-being in my career?
- What opportunities for growth and advancement do I see in my current job or field?
- How do I navigate professional relationships and interactions with colleagues, supervisors, and clients?
- What steps can I take to enhance my skills or qualifications in my chosen field?
- What professional development opportunities or resources do I seek out or utilize?
- How do I handle setbacks or failures in my career, and what do I learn from them?
- What are my long-term career aspirations and dreams?

- How do I define success and fulfillment in my professional life?
- What strategies do I use to manage stress and maintain resilience in my career?
- What role do networking and building professional relationships play in my career development?
- How do I stay motivated and inspired in my professional pursuits?
- What are my strategies for managing time and priorities effectively in my work?
- How do I advocate for myself and my career goals within my organization or industry?
- How do I envision my professional journey evolving in the future?

* * *

UNLOCK THE POWER OF YOUR GENEROSITY

"To the world, you may be one person, but to one person, you may be the world."
— Dr. Seuss

Helping others makes us happier, healthier, and even more successful. If we can make a difference together, why not try it?

So, here's a question for you...

Would you help someone you've never met, even if you never got credit for it?

That person may be like you, or maybe like you used to be. They may be struggling with stress and anxiety, overwhelmed, nearing burnout, and have no idea where to turn. They may just need a bit of help, but don't know where to start.

While struggling to overcome trauma, grief, and loss, and simultaneously clawing my way back to health, the self-care resources I compiled in *The Ultimate Self-Care Handbook: 1000+ Hassle-Free Ideas to Escape Burnout, Reduce Stress, and Reclaim Your Life* served as my compass, paving the way for me to reclaim my life. Now that I'm on the other side, I feel a deep responsibility to share those resources with others and help ease the suffering of as many people as possible.

Most people judge a book by its cover (and its reviews). So here's my ask - on behalf of all the folks struggling with their trauma, loss, grief, or those who feel burdened by a chronic sense of overwhelm – for all those you've never met:

Please help those struggling to find wellness by leaving a review for this book.

This book will only reach the people who need it with your help. This one small act costs no money and takes less than 60 seconds, but it can create a ripple of positivity within the world.

I wouldn't be true to myself if I didn't weave into this ask, all the self-care benefits you can personally experience from doing good things for others. Scientific evidence suggests that altruistic behaviors:

- Increases the production of serotonin, endorphins, and oxytocin - hormones promoting happiness and relaxation.
- Blood pressure is naturally lowered through acts of kindness that benefit the heart.
- Pro-social behaviors are linked to decreases in depression and improved immune function.
- An increased sense of well-being, stress reduction, and improved mental health.
- A greater sense of belonging, self-esteem and community.

To get that 'feel good' feeling, tap into the benefits of your own self-care, and help this person for real. All you have to do is…and it takes less than 60 seconds…

Leave a review.

Scan the QR code above to review the paperback or click here to review the e-book.

If you feel good about helping someone you don't know, you are my kind of person. Welcome to the club. You're one of us. Thank you for taking quick action to get this into the hands of those in need.

You're empowered by the self-assessment you just took and you know where you want to start exploring new ways to bring balance into your life. I'm really excited to share all the tips and resources in the coming chapters.

Thank you from the bottom of my heart. Now, back to our regularly scheduled program.

Your biggest fan, Lorilee

"As we work to create light for others, we naturally light our own way."
— **Mary Anne Radmacher**

8

FINANCIAL SELF-CARE

"Taking control of your finances is an act of self-care.
It's about valuing yourself and your future." - Unknown

F inancial self-care is crucial for overall well-being as
it empowers individuals to make informed financial
decisions, reduce stress, and achieve financial goals.
By practicing financial self-care, individuals can manage their
money effectively, build financial security, and cultivate a sense
of economic stability.

Your Relationship with Money

Understand your "money story" or your "money script."
Your beliefs may hold you back until you understand your
relationship to money and your unconscious thoughts about
becoming wealthy. Journalling about the topic of money,
abundance, and prosperity in non-monetary value systems
and the memories you have about what money meant in your
childhood home will help you to uncover the belief systems

and meanings attached to money that are operating in the background of your subconscious mind. Working with a financial coach is another great way to access these beliefs and start to reshape and reframe the story you'd like to consciously develop to launch yourself on the path to financial freedom, legacy wealth, and lifelong giving.

Create a Budget

Use the **50/30/20 rule** to allocate your income effectively. The **50/30/20 plan** is a simple yet effective budgeting framework designed to help you manage your finances with clarity and balance. By dividing your after-tax income into three categories—50% for needs, 30% for wants, and 20% for savings and debt repayment—this plan ensures that your essential expenses are covered while leaving room for enjoyment and long-term financial goals. Its straightforward approach makes it an excellent starting point for anyone looking to take control of their financial well-being. **50% for Needs:**

Allocate half of your income to essential expenses. These are necessary costs required for survival and maintaining your standard of living. Examples include:

- Housing (rent or mortgage payments)
- Utilities (electricity, water, heating)
- Groceries
- Transportation (gas, car payments, public transit)
- Insurance (health, auto, home)
- Minimum debt payments

30% for Wants:

Spend 30% of your income on discretionary expenses—

things you enjoy but can live without. These include:

- Dining out
- Entertainment (movies, concerts, hobbies)
- Shopping for non-essential items
- Vacations
- Subscription services (streaming platforms, gym memberships)

20% for Savings and Debt Repayment:
Direct 20% of your income toward financial goals and improve your future financial health. This includes:

- Building an emergency fund
- Investing in retirement accounts (e.g., 401(k), IRA)
- Paying off high-interest debt faster than required
- Saving for major future expenses (e.g., a house, education, or a car)

Strategies for Building a Stable Financial Future

- **Pay Off Debt:** High-interest debt, such as credit cards and personal loans, should be your top priority. Develop a structured repayment plan using either the debt avalanche method (tackling the highest interest rates first) or the debt snowball method (starting with the smallest balance). Once debt-free, redirect funds previously used for debt payments into savings or investments to accelerate wealth-building.
- **Build an Emergency Fund:** Save enough to cover three to six months of living expenses to protect against un-

expected events like job loss or medical emergencies. Use a high-yield savings account for better returns while maintaining liquidity. Keep this fund separate from daily spending to ensure it's available when truly needed.

- **Automate Savings:** Automate contributions to savings accounts, retirement plans, and investment portfolios to ensure consistency and reduce spending temptation. Automatic transfers make financial discipline easier by treating savings as a non-negotiable.
- **Invest for the Long Term:** Start early and contribute regularly to retirement accounts like 401(k)s, IRAs, Roth IRAs, or SEP IRAs (for self-employed individuals). Take advantage of employer-sponsored plans by contributing enough to earn matching benefits. Diversify your portfolio with a mix of stocks, bonds, and other assets aligned with your risk tolerance and financial goals.
- **Diversify Investments:** Spread investments across asset classes (e.g., equities, bonds, real estate), industries, and geographic regions to minimize risk. Consider index funds or ETFs for broad market exposure with low fees. Avoid holding excess cash and keep liquid assets, like emergency funds, in high-yield savings accounts for better returns.
- **Tax Planning:** Use tax-efficient strategies to maximize savings
- Contribute to Health Savings Accounts (HSAs) for medical expenses while enjoying triple tax benefits (tax-free contributions, growth, and withdrawals).
- Optimize retirement contributions to lower taxable income.
- Claim deductions and credits are available to homeowners,

parents, or small business owners.

- **Save for Children's Education:** Consider tax-advantaged accounts like a 529 plan or Coverdell ESA for education savings. These accounts offer tax benefits and flexible investment options to support your children's future. Encourage them to apply for scholarships, grants, and other financial aid to reduce education costs.

- **Pay Off Your Home:** Reduce mortgage debt faster by making extra payments toward the principal, switching to biweekly payments, or rounding up to the nearest hundred dollars. Use financial windfalls, such as tax refunds or bonuses, to make lump-sum payments. Monitor mortgage rates for refinancing opportunities, ensuring there are no prepayment penalties before making additional contributions.

- **Protect Financial Stability with Insurance:** Adequate coverage is essential to safeguarding your financial future. Ensure you have:

- Health insurance to protect against medical emergencies.
- Life insurance to provide for dependents.
- Disability insurance to maintain income during unexpected health challenges.
- Home and auto insurance to protect valuable assets.

- **Legacy and Estate Planning:** Plan for the future by creating a will or trust to ensure your assets are distributed according to your wishes. Designate beneficiaries for retirement accounts and insurance policies. Consider consulting with an estate planner to address tax implications and protect generational wealth.

- **Build Wealth and Give Back:** Once you've eliminated debt, established investments, and ensured financial stability, focus on growing wealth. Diversify investments further, explore new opportunities, and set aside funds for philanthropy. Giving to causes that matter to you can be a fulfilling way to share your success while making a positive impact.

Money Mindset

Maintaining a positive money mindset is essential for managing finances effectively and achieving financial well-being. How you think about money impacts your financial decisions and the stress or fulfillment you experience in managing your resources. Cultivating a healthy and intentional relationship with money involves awareness, forgiveness, and a commitment to growth.

- **Avoid Comparison:** Resist the urge to compare your financial situation with others. This can lead to feelings of inadequacy, discontent, or overwhelm. Instead, stay focused on your own journey, set realistic goals, and take small steps to improve your situation.
- **Forgive Financial Mistakes:** Acknowledge past financial missteps without judgment and forgive yourself. Every mistake offers a valuable lesson. Commit to healthier habits to maximize your future success, stability, and financial health.
- **Practice Mindful Spending:** Develop healthy spending habits by distinguishing between needs and wants. Practice moderation, delay gratification, and avoid impulse purchases or falling for urgency-driven sales tactics. Spend intentionally, knowing your needs, and prevent regrets by aligning purchases with your values.

- **Celebrate Financial Wins:** Recognize and celebrate milestones, whether big or small. Whether paying off a credit card, reaching a savings goal, sticking to a budget, or negotiating a raise, acknowledging your progress reinforces positive behaviors and builds momentum.
- **Focus on Your Values:** Align your financial choices with your core values and long-term goals. This will ensure that your spending, saving, and investing decisions reflect what truly matters to you rather than fleeting desires or societal pressures.
- **Aim for an Abundant Mindset:** Shift from a scarcity mindset to one of abundance. Believe that there are unlimited resources and opportunities available to everyone. By focusing on possibilities and using confirmation bias to your advantage, you'll naturally attract and recognize opportunities to grow your wealth.
- **Gratitude for Resources:** Cultivate gratitude for the financial resources you already have, no matter the amount. Recognizing small financial blessings can shift your perspective, reduce anxiety, and increase your confidence in managing money.
- **Reframe Limiting Beliefs:** Identify negative thoughts about money, such as "I'll never have enough" or "Money is the root of all evil." Replace them with empowering affirmations like, "I am capable of creating financial security" or "Money is a tool to create opportunities and support others."
- **Visualize Financial Goals:** Imagine your financial success vividly, whether it's becoming debt-free, achieving a savings goal, or creating generational wealth. Visualization keeps goals tangible, motivates action, and reinforces the

belief that success is achievable.

- **Understand Money as Energy:** View money as a dynamic flow of energy, not a static resource. It moves in and out as you exchange value with the world. This perspective can reduce the fear of spending while encouraging thoughtful and intentional financial decisions.
- **Detach Self-Worth from Net Worth:** Remember that your value as a person is not tied to the amount of money you have. Financial ups and downs are a natural part of life, and your worth remains constant regardless of your bank balance.
- **Embrace Lifelong Learning:** Commit to improving your financial literacy by reading books, attending workshops, or using online resources. Financial knowledge empowers you to make informed decisions and builds confidence in managing money.
- **Surround Yourself with Positivity:** Spend time with people who have healthy financial habits and a growth-oriented mindset. Positive influences can inspire constructive approaches to money management and encourage you to focus on your goals.
- **Be Patient with Growth:** Financial success is a journey, not an overnight transformation. Progress happens incrementally, so celebrate small victories and view setbacks as opportunities for growth.
- By cultivating a positive money mindset, you can build a healthier relationship with money, reduce stress, and open yourself to greater financial possibilities. Your financial goals can become a reality with intention, patience, and persistence.

Take Financial Assessments

For those interested in additional exploration, you may take additional assessments to gauge your financial health. You can seek out these resources with an internet search.

- Financial Personality Assessment
- Financial Well-Being Assessment
- Money Habitudes Assessment

Journal Prompts for Financial Health and Well-Being

- What was the general attitude about money like in the home where you grew up?
- What was the attitude around spending money?
- What was the feeling around saving money?
- What was the viewpoint around giving money away?
- What's your earliest money memory?
- What beliefs did your mother pass down to you about money?
- What beliefs did your father pass down to you about money?
- Do you remember hearing your parents talk about (or fight about) money?
- Did you have more than/less than/about the same as your peers?
- What are my current financial goals, both short-term and long-term?
- How do I feel about my current financial situation?
- What are my attitudes and beliefs about money and wealth?
- What are my sources of income, and how do I manage them?

125

- What are my regular expenses, and how do I budget for them?
- What debts do I have, if any, and how do I plan to manage or pay them off?
- What are my savings and investment strategies?
- How do I track my financial progress and goals?
- What are my financial strengths and areas for improvement?
- What financial risks or uncertainties must I address or plan for?
- How do I align spending and saving with my values and goals?
- What steps can I take to increase my income or improve my financial situation?
- What financial habits or behaviors do I want to change or develop?
- How do I manage financial stress or anxiety?
- What role does financial education play in my financial decision-making?
- How do I plan for major expenses or financial milestones, such as buying a home or retiring?
- What are my strategies for protecting and growing my wealth over time?
- How do I involve my family or loved ones in financial planning and decision-making?
- What are my long-term financial aspirations and dreams?
- How do I define financial success and fulfillment in my life?

9

INTELLECTUAL SELF-CARE

"In learning, you will teach, and in teaching, you will learn."
- Phil Collins

I ntellectual self-care involves exploring new ideas, challenging beliefs, and broadening perspectives to foster personal growth and self-awareness. Engaging in activities like learning, problem-solving, and critical thinking activates neuroplasticity, the brain's ability to reorganize and form new connections. These activities release neurotransmitters, such as dopamine and glutamate, which strengthen synaptic pathways and support overall brain health.

Intellectual stimulation can enhance cognitive abilities, improve memory retention, and protect against cognitive decline. Intellectual self-care promotes lifelong learning and ensures quality and longevity by building mental resilience and adaptability.

Understand your Learning Style

Learning style inventories assess an individual's preferred approaches to learning and processing information. While not explicitly focused on intellectual stimulation, understanding one's learning style can help identify strategies for intellectual engagement and growth best suited to an individual's preferences and strengths.

- **Visual Learners:** Visual learners prefer to learn through visual stimuli such as images, diagrams, charts, and videos. They benefit from seeing information presented in a graphical or spatial format and may use visual aids to organize and remember information.
- **Auditory Learners:** Auditory learners learn best through auditory stimuli such as lectures, discussions, verbal explanations, and recorded materials. They prefer to listen to information rather than read or see it and may benefit from using verbal repetition or mnemonic devices to reinforce learning.
- **Read/Write Learners:** Read/write learners prefer to learn through written or textual materials such as books, articles, handouts, and written instructions. They excel at reading and writing tasks and may like to take notes or create written summaries to process and retain information.
- **Kinesthetic/Tactile Learners:** Kinesthetic or tactile learners learn best through hands-on experiences, physical activities, and movement. They prefer engaging with materials through touch, manipulation, and physical interaction. They may also benefit from experiments, demonstrations, or role-playing exercises.

Intellectual Practices for Growth

1. Engage in Intellectual Discussions

Join book clubs, debate teams, or study circles to engage in stimulating conversations and exchange ideas with others. Philosophical debates can challenge our thinking and give us new perspectives and worldviews. Through intellectual discussions, we can gain insights into the lens we see the world through and aim to put on another person's lens to view it differently. Surrounding ourselves with only people who share our belief systems is the surest way to keep a small worldview. Engaging with others encourages us to consider things we may not have considered before and helps refine or change our beliefs.

2. Critical Thinking Exercises

Practice critical thinking by engaging in activities that require analysis, evaluation, and problem-solving.

- Participate in brainstorming sessions to explore unconventional solutions.
- Analyze data sets or statistics to draw meaningful conclusions.
- Review case studies or public policy to understand complex scenarios and develop informed opinions.
- Play strategic games like chess or modern group activities like escape rooms to practice decision-making and collaborative problem-solving.

3. Lifelong Learning

Lifelong learning profoundly affects the brain and neurons,

leading to structural and functional changes that enhance cognitive function, memory, and overall brain health. Commit to consistently seeking opportunities to learn new skills, information, concepts, and perspectives. The health benefits are incredible.

- **Neuroplasticity:** Lifelong learning promotes neuroplasticity, the brain's ability to reorganize itself by forming new neural connections throughout life. When individuals engage in learning activities, such as studying, problem-solving, or acquiring new skills, they stimulate the growth of new synapses and strengthen existing neural pathways. This enhances neural communication and improves cognitive function.
- **Synaptic Pruning:** Lifelong learning also involves synaptic pruning, eliminating unused or less efficient neural connections to streamline neural networks. Through education and cognitive stimulation, the brain identifies and strengthens the most relevant and efficient neural pathways while eliminating redundant or unnecessary connections. This optimizes brain function and enhances cognitive efficiency.
- **Neurogenesis:** Lifelong learning has been shown to stimulate neurogenesis, the process of generating new neurons in the brain. Learning activities that are mentally challenging and intellectually stimulating, such as reading, problem-solving, and learning new skills, promote the production of new neurons in the hippocampus, a brain region involved in learning and memory. This contributes to cognitive flexibility, memory formation, and overall brain health.

- **Improved Cognitive Function:** Lifelong learning enhances cognitive function by sharpening attention, improving memory, and boosting executive function skills such as problem-solving, decision-making, and planning. Engaging in mentally stimulating activities keeps the brain active and agile, helping to reduce the risk of cognitive decline with age.
- **Enhanced Neuroprotective Mechanisms:** Lifelong learning activates neuroprotective mechanisms that help protect the brain from damage and degeneration. Learning activities stimulate the production of neurotrophic factors, such as brain-derived neurotrophic factor (BDNF), which promote neuronal survival, growth, and repair. These neuroprotective factors help preserve brain health and resilience, reducing the risk of neurodegenerative diseases such as Alzheimer's and Parkinson's.

Ideas for Lifelong Learning

- **Explore Different Perspectives:** To broaden your understanding and cultivate empathy, seek diverse viewpoints and perspectives on various topics. Read books, watch documentaries, or converse with people from different backgrounds and cultures.
- **Attending Lectures and Talks:** To expand your knowledge and expose yourself to new ideas and insights, attend public lectures, seminars, or TED talks on topics of interest. Many educational institutions, libraries, and cultural organizations offer public lectures and events open to the community.

- **Mind Mapping:** Use mind mapping techniques to organize and brainstorm ideas, concepts, and connections visually. Mind maps can help clarify thoughts, plan projects, and stimulate creative thinking.
- **Set Goals:** Establish clear and achievable goals that align with your values, interests, and aspirations. Break down larger goals into smaller, actionable steps, and regularly review your progress to stay on track.
- **Seek New Experiences:** Step outside your comfort zone and embrace opportunities for learning and growth. Try new activities, explore different interests, and challenge yourself to expand your horizons and develop new skills.
- **Reflect Regularly:** Set aside dedicated time for self-reflection daily, weekly, or monthly. Use journaling, meditation, or quiet contemplation to reflect on your thoughts, feelings, experiences, and goals.
- **Seek Inspiration:** Surround yourself with people who inspire and motivate you to be your best self. Connect with mentors, role models, or peers who share your values and aspirations, and draw inspiration from their experiences and achievements.
- **Embrace Failure:** Embrace failure as a natural part of the learning process and an opportunity for growth. Learn from your mistakes, adapt your approach, and persevere while facing challenges.
- **Teach Others:** Share your knowledge and expertise through mentoring, tutoring, or teaching opportunities. Teaching is an effective way to reinforce your own learning and deepen your understanding of a subject.

Digital Tools and Community Resources

Leverage modern resources to make intellectual self-care accessible:

- **Apps for Learning and Brain Training:** Use tools like Duolingo (language learning), Lumosity (brain training), or Skillshare (creative skills) to engage your mind.
- **Online Courses:** Platforms like Coursera, Udemy, Lynda or MasterClass provide opportunities to learn from experts in various fields. Alternative platforms such as MindValley or Gaia have an extremely diverse array of video coursework to expand your perspectives.
- **Local Opportunities:** To connect with others and explore new ideas, participate in community-based events like library programs, public lectures, or cultural workshops.

Balance is key to intellectual self-care. While stimulating your mind through learning and critical thinking is vital, creating space for rest and recovery ensures integration and mental clarity. By making intellectual self-care a regular practice, you enhance your ability to navigate life's challenges with curiosity, resilience, and adaptability. Engage your mind, explore new horizons, and embrace the joy of learning for a lifetime.

Journal Prompts for Intellectual Health and Well-Being

- What subjects or topics am I most passionate about intellectually?
- How do I engage my intellect in my daily life?
- What books, articles, or podcasts have inspired me recently?

- What questions or puzzles am I currently exploring or seeking answers to?
- How do I challenge myself intellectually and continue to grow?
- What role does critical thinking play in my intellectual pursuits?
- What areas of knowledge or skills do I want to develop further?
- How do I stay informed and engaged with current events and global issues?
- What intellectual hobbies or activities do I enjoy?
- What opportunities do I have to learn and acquire new knowledge or skills?
- How do I seek out diverse perspectives and opinions on different topics?
- What intellectual challenges or obstacles do I face, and how do I overcome them?
- How do I apply my intellect to problem-solving and decision-making?
- What role does creativity play in my intellectual pursuits?
- What historical figures or thought leaders do I admire or find inspiring?
- How do I balance my intellectual pursuits with other aspects of my life?
- How do I use intellectual activities to reduce stress or gain clarity?
- What steps can I take to balance intellectual stimulation with rest?
- How do I stay curious and open to new perspectives?
- What opportunities do I have to engage in intellectual discussions or debates?

10

SPIRITUAL SELF-CARE

*"Your sacred space is where you can find yourself
over and over again." - Joseph Campbell*

Spirituality is a deeply personal and subjective experience. For some, it is closely tied to religious or cultural traditions, involving practices like attending services, studying sacred texts, or participating in rituals or ceremonies. For others, spirituality may be found in the awe of nature, quiet introspection, or the pursuit of meaning and purpose.

Spiritual self-care involves exploring the deeper questions of life—our purpose, the nature of existence, and our connection to the universe. It allows us to access our authentic selves, align with our values, and navigate life with a sense of fulfillment. By integrating rituals, introspection, and acts of service, spiritual self-care can foster resilience, compassion and a sense of secure inner knowing of who we are and our connection to the universe as a whole.

Exploring Beliefs and Values

Understanding and aligning with one's belief system is fundamental to spiritual self-care. Beliefs are not fixed truths or absolute certainties. They are personal choices that evolve as one gains new insights, reflects on one's experiences, and clarifies one's values. While beliefs are neither inherently right nor wrong, they play a powerful role in shaping one's sense of purpose, guiding one's actions, and influencing one's fulfillment.

Spiritual self-care begins with exploring and cultivating the beliefs, values, and practices that bring meaning and connection to one's life. Living in alignment with one's core beliefs can lead to a sense of ease, peace, and authenticity. The rituals and practices one integrates into one's life should connect one more wholly to one's true self—the raw, unfiltered expression of who one is meant to be and what one is here to offer the world.

Assessing and Deepening Your Beliefs

To clarify your values and beliefs, consider engaging with tools and practices that encourage self-reflection and mindfulness. Assessments can provide valuable insights into your sense of purpose and well-being. You can take Mindfulness and Spiritual Assessment Tests by searching for these tests online:

- **Spiritual Well-Being Scale (SWBS):** Measures an individual's overall sense of spiritual health and connection, focusing on existential and religious well-being.
- **Faith Maturity Scale (FMS):** Designed to assess faith maturity regarding beliefs, values, and practices, particularly

for those from religious backgrounds.

- **Belief in a Just World Scale (BJWS):** Explores how strongly someone believes that the world operates fairly and justly, influencing spiritual and moral perspectives.
- **Spiritual Transformation Scale (STS):** This scale examines personal transformation in spiritual beliefs, especially after significant life events or challenges.
- **Spiritual Intelligence Self-Report Inventory (SISRI-24):** Measures spiritual intelligence, including personal meaning-making, transcendence, and conscious alignment with one's values.
- The **PERMA Profiler** to evaluate positive emotions, engagement, relationships, meaning, and accomplishment.

Cultivating a Sense of Purpose

Finding spiritual purpose isn't about solving the mysteries of life but appreciating its richness and discovering how your unique qualities contribute to the greater good. Some individuals feel a clear calling toward a specific cause, occupation, or ministry, while others uncover their purpose gradually through quiet reflection and practice.

Through spiritual self-care, you can connect more deeply with your whole self and use your talents to create positivity in the world. The most significant outcome of spiritual practice is self-actualization—consciously stepping into your inherent gifts, talents, and hard-wiring and sharing them with the world. By aligning your daily actions with your beliefs and values, you ignite passion and joy in your own life while profoundly enriching the lives of those around you.

Developing Your Belief System

137

Beliefs require trust, faith, and a willingness to embrace the unknown. They are not based on irrefutable facts but on deeply personal choices that reflect one's inner truth. As one evolves, one's beliefs may shift in response to new experiences, knowledge, or insights. This adaptability allows one to refine one's understanding of what brings meaning and purpose to one's life.

To deepen your understanding of your belief system, reflect on these key questions:

- What gives my life meaning and purpose?
- What does it mean to me to be a good person?
- What are my non-negotiables for living authentically?
- How do I find comfort during times of sorrow or adversity?
- What role do free will and destiny play in my understanding of life events?
- What values guide my decisions and actions?
- How do I remain open to others' beliefs, even when they differ from mine?
- What is my perspective on consciousness, energy, and life force?
- What do I believe happens after death, and how do those beliefs shape my approach to life?
- What is the relationship between mind, body, and spirit in shaping the human experience?

Engage in Rituals and Reflective Practices

Deepening your spiritual self-care involves regular rituals that quiet the mind and allow you to reconnect with your beliefs and values. These practices don't need to be elaborate— their purpose is to create a sacred space where you can reflect, align, and grow. Personal rituals hold meaning for you or help you to pause and find peace within your mind for safe reflection. The rituals themselves are less important than their ability to help you access and create a sacred space to experience a connection to the divine (whatever that means for you).

Establishing rituals to which you attach personal meaning can be a powerful way to invite the spirit to guide you. Consider some of the rituals below to create a quiet, sacred space for reflection. This can be an excellent time to ponder some of the existential thoughts listed above in an intentional way.

- **Burn candles:** Use their glow as a focal point for meditation or prayer.
- **Light incense:** Engage your senses and create a calming atmosphere.
- **Create an altar:** Incorporate natural elements like leaves, rocks, or sticks to personalize your sacred space.
- **Rake a sand garden:** This mindful activity promotes inner calm and clarity.
- **Read from a holy text:** Reflect on passages that resonate with your values and beliefs.
- **Listen to peaceful music:** Allow soothing sounds to guide your thoughts inward.
- **Pull an oracle or affirmation card:** Use it as a starting point for self-reflection.
- **Pray or meditate:** Create stillness and connect to your inner self or higher power.
- **Use guided imagery or breathwork:** Visualize tranquility or focus on your breath to ground yourself.

- **Express gratitude:** Write "Thank you" in the sand, dirt, or journal to acknowledge life's blessings.
- **Observe nature:** Spend time watching the flow of a brook, the rustling of leaves, or the dance of wildlife.
- **Incorporate symbolic tools:** Use mala beads, rosaries, or hand mudras to deepen your practice.

Volunteer or Serve Others

Acts of service are a profound way to nurture spiritual self-care. Volunteering fosters compassion reinforces interconnectedness, and helps align actions with values. You embody kindness, empathy, and selflessness through service, uplifting yourself and your community.

Generosity has a unique power to lift us out of personal struggles by creating meaningful connections and fostering a sense of purpose. Allowing your time and energy to be a conduit for good elevates your spirit and strengthens community bonds. Service also combats feelings of isolation, depression, and loneliness, creating a sense of belonging.

Ways to Serve:

- **Soup kitchen or food bank:** Serve meals or help distribute food to those in need at a local soup kitchen or food bank.
- **Homeless shelter:** Volunteer at a homeless shelter by assisting with meal preparation, serving food, or providing support to residents.
- **Create Homeless Care Packages:** Get creative and put together seasonal or gender-specific care packages to support homeless people. Warm blankets, socks, hygiene

items, gift cards, snacks, etc., along with a sweet, uplifting note, can make someone's life a little easier.

- **Animal shelter:** Volunteer at an animal shelter by walking dogs, socializing with cats, or helping with cleaning and maintenance tasks.
- **Hospital or nursing home:** Volunteer at a hospital or nursing home by visiting patients, assisting with activities, or providing companionship to residents.
- **Tutoring or mentoring:** Volunteer as a tutor or mentor to children or adults needing academic support or guidance.
- **Environmental cleanup:** Participate in community clean-up efforts by planting trees or maintaining local parks and trails. Get involved with graffiti removal programs and highway or Beach clean-up events.
- **Disaster relief:** Volunteer with organizations that provide disaster relief assistance, such as distributing supplies or offering emotional support to affected communities.
- **Community garden:** Volunteers can help maintain a community garden by planting, weeding, watering, or harvesting produce for residents.
- **Literacy programs:** Volunteer with literacy programs or adult education centers to help individuals improve their reading, writing, or English language skills.
- **Senior services:** You can assist seniors in your community by running errands, providing transportation, making minor home repairs, or offering companionship through programs like Meals on Wheels or senior centers.
- **Youth programs:** Volunteer with youth programs, such as after-school programs, sports teams, or youth clubs, to mentor and support young people.

- **Community events:** Volunteer at community events, festivals, or fundraisers by helping with set-up, clean-up, registration, or coordination.
- **Crisis hotline:** Volunteer for a crisis hotline or support service to provide emotional support and resources to individuals in crisis or distress.
- **Blood donation:** Donate blood or volunteer at blood drives to support healthcare organizations and help save lives.
- **Prison outreach:** Volunteer with organizations that provide support and rehabilitation services to individuals in prisons or detention centers.
- **Refugee resettlement:** Volunteer with refugee resettlement agencies to assist refugees with finding housing, accessing resources, and adjusting to their new community.
- **Community education:** Offer to teach a class or workshop on a topic of interest to your community, such as financial literacy, gardening, or cooking.
- **Virtual volunteering:** Explore opportunities for virtual volunteering, such as online tutoring, social media management for nonprofit organizations, or virtual mentoring programs.
- **Community advocacy:** Get involved in community advocacy efforts by volunteering with organizations that address social justice issues, advocate for policy change, or promote equality and inclusion in your community.
- **Share fundraiser pages:** Be a conduit for connecting folks with causes that are important to you with folks who have money to spare.
- **Donate your Stuff:** We all have more than we need these days, and it's a simple act to reduce clutter in our own

homes while simultaneously providing for those in need.

Journal Prompts for Spiritual Health and Well-Being

- What does spirituality mean to me?
- What values or beliefs are essential to my spiritual well-being?
- How do I connect with my inner self or higher power?
- What practices or rituals help me feel grounded and connected spiritually?
- How do I approach challenges or setbacks from a spiritual perspective?
- What role does gratitude play in my spiritual life?
- How do I cultivate mindfulness and presence in my daily life?
- What inspires me or fills me with a sense of awe and wonder?
- How do I nurture compassion and kindness towards myself and others?
- What lessons or insights have I gained from past spiritual experiences?
- How do I integrate my spiritual principles into my relationships and interactions with others?
- What role does forgiveness play in my spiritual journey?
- How do I align my daily actions with my spiritual values and beliefs?
- What fears or obstacles do I face in deepening my spiritual practice, and how can I overcome them?
- How do I honor and celebrate the sacredness of life in ordinary moments?
- What practices help me cultivate inner peace and harmony,

even during stressful times?

- How do I remain open to others' spiritual beliefs that differ from mine?
- What spiritual practices bring me the most joy or clarity, and why?
- How do I cultivate trust and surrender during times of uncertainty or challenge?
- What are my intentions for growth and transformation on my spiritual path?

11

RECREATIONAL SELF-CARE

"We don't stop playing because we grow old; we grow old because we stop playing." - George Bernard Shaw

R ecreation and play are essential components of a balanced self-care routine. They create space for relaxation, rejuvenation, and joy, counteracting the stress and busyness of modern life. Engaging in recreational activities stimulates the release of endorphins—your body's feel-good chemicals—boosting happiness, improving energy, and fostering an overall sense of well-being. This simple bio-hack uses our body's innate chemistry to reduce stress naturally and helps us to mentally and physically unwind. Many recreational activities offer opportunities to foster social connections and strengthen relationships, compounding the "feel-good" hormone release throughout the body.

In today's hustle culture, recreation is often dismissed as unproductive or indulgent. Many of us tie our self-worth to productivity, a mindset instilled early through social and cultural conditioning. However, research shows that prioritizing play and recreation has measurable physiological, emotional, and social benefits. Through activities that promote curiosity, laughter, fun, and adventure, we can enhance creativity, improve mood, increase energy levels, and foster deeper connections with others. The net benefit is clear - play brings a vast improvement in the quality of life.

Understanding your "Playful Personality Type"

Knowing your playful personality type can guide you toward activities that align with your preferences, ensuring a more fulfilling experience. Here are four common playful personality types and corresponding activity suggestions:

1. Other-Oriented: Enjoys bringing joy to others through shared activities.

- Suggested Activities: Team sports, cooperative games, group volunteering, or hosting game nights.

2. Intellectual: Thrives on curiosity, creativity, and mental stimulation.

- Suggested Activities: Strategy games, trivia nights, escape rooms, or learning-based hobbies like coding or solving puzzles.

3. Whimsical: Embraces spontaneity, novelty, and imagination.

- Suggested Activities: Improv classes, treasure hunts, quirky art projects, or trying unconventional activities like goat yoga.

4. Lighthearted: Seeks fun, laughter, and carefree enjoyment.

- Suggested Activities: Comedy shows, karaoke, board games, or outdoor games like cornhole or pickleball.

Recreation and Play: Ideas for Fun and Relaxation
Recreation encompasses activities engaged in purely for leisure, relaxation, or enjoyment. These moments allow us to unwind, connect with others, and rediscover a sense of playfulness. An individual's tastes and preferences dictate whether that activity will achieve enjoyment.

1. **Schedule Leisure Time:**

- **Prioritize Recreation**: Block off dedicated time for leisure and treat it as non-negotiable. Taking play seriously is a vital part of self-care.
- **Stay Flexible**: Allow your mood and energy levels to guide your choice of activities during your leisure time.

2. Outdoor Adventures

- **Spend Time in Nature**: Recharge with a walk in the park, a hike, or a picnic. Watch a sunset by a lake or enjoy fresh air in a tranquil spot..
- **Plan Hobby-Based Trips**: Create a trip centered on your hobbies, such as fishing, photography, biking, or kayaking.
- **Go on Themed Road Trips**: Explore ghost towns, soak in hot springs, or visit factory tours for a unique adventure.
- **Tour Your Hometown**: Experience your area like a

tourist—visit local attractions, historical sites, or hidden gems with fresh eyes.

3. Creative Pursuits

- **Explore Hobbies**: Pursue creative outlets such as painting, gardening, knitting, or writing.
- **Try Something New**: Attend pottery classes, calligraphy workshops, or sip-and-paint events to broaden your creative horizons.
- **Rediscover Childhood Creativity**: Build with LEGO, color in adult coloring books, or doodle whimsical designs for fun.

4. Childlike Play

- **Revisit Childhood Favorites**: Blow bubbles, build blanket forts, start a pillow fight, or play outdoor games like tag and hide-and-seek.
- **Play Dress-Up**: Experiment with costumes, wigs, or accessories to embrace your playful alter ego. Host a small party where these items are accessible for impromptu play.
- **Create Silly Moments**: Doodle on Post-it notes and leave them in unexpected places, such as co-workers' desks or public mirrors, to create surprise; snap pictures of yourself making funny faces and randomly send to family or friends.

5. Social Recreation

- **Host Game Nights**: Gather friends or family for board

games, card games, trivia, or even life-sized Jenga.

- **Dance and Sing**: Crank up your favorite tunes and have a spontaneous dance party, or try karaoke with a group.
- **Connect Through Laughter**: Explore laughter yoga, attend a comedy show, or share jokes to strengthen social bonds and lift your spirits.

6. Novelty and Adventure

- **Try Something Different**: Step out of your comfort zone with activities like horseback riding, axe throwing, or disc golf.
- **Explore Unique Experiences**: To keep life exciting, participate in unconventional activities such as goat yoga, treasure hunts, or geocaching.
- **Say "Yes" to Spontaneity**: Infuse your days with adventure by embracing unexpected opportunities for fun.

Play is a spontaneous and voluntary activity done purely for the joy it brings, without any external purpose or expectation. It is about embracing creativity, freedom of expression, and moments of uninhibited fun. Whether through imaginative play, role-playing, or acts of silliness and humor, play reconnects us with our sense of wonder and joy. While there are endless ideas and resources to inspire play, the best moments often come from spontaneous opportunities where you say, "Why not?" So let yourself be playful, be goofy, and rediscover the simple pleasures that make life lighter and brighter.

To help you reflect on your relationship with play and how to incorporate more of it into your life, consider the following journal prompts:

Journal Prompts for Recreational Health and Well-Being

- What activities bring me joy and excitement?
- When was the last time I felt playful and carefree? What was I doing?
- How do I prioritize fun and leisure in my daily routine?
- What hobbies or creative outlets have I always wanted to try?
- How do humor and laughter contribute to my sense of well-being?
- What childhood activities did I love that I could revisit now?
- How do I feel when I'm fully immersed in play or creative expression?
- What role do social connections play in my recreational activities?
- How do I balance work, responsibilities, and recreation?
- How can I infuse more spontaneity and adventure into my daily life?
- What limiting beliefs or self-judgments prevent me from embracing recreation?
- How can I create an environment that encourages creativity and playfulness?
- What new experiences or adventures could I explore?
- What small, simple pleasures consistently bring me happiness?
- How do I recharge when I feel mentally or emotionally drained?
- What inspires me to try new activities or step outside my comfort zone?
- How do I ensure my playtime is free of external pressures,

like social media?
- How can I incorporate more novelty and variety into my recreational activities?
- What creative or playful activity could I try today just for myself?
- How do I honor the value of play in my life without guilt or hesitation?

12

ENVIRONMENTAL SELF-CARE

"Outer order contributes to inner calm." - Gretchen Rubin

Whether managing the personal space of our home, car, office, garage, or yard, it is an integral part of self-care because it directly impacts our physical, emotional, and mental well-being. Living spaces are the backdrop for our daily lives and greatly influence our mood, energy levels, comfort, and security.A well-maintained and personalized environment promotes relaxation, reduces stress, and enhances our ability to function effectively. It creates ease and efficiency in daily operations and gives us a creative outlet for expressing our personality, preferences, tastes, and desires. Environmental self-care involves intentionally creating a space that reflects who we are and fosters comfort, peace, and rejuvenation. By aligning our surroundings with our needs and preferences, we can cultivate a sanctuary that supports rest and renewal.

Cleaning and Decluttering

The most apparent aspect of environmental self-care is keeping your living, workspaces, and vehicle physically clean. Regularly decluttering these spaces creates a sense of order and calm. Clearing out unnecessary items reduces visual distractions and promotes a more organized environment. Use the "keep, donate, or discard" method to systematically go through your belongings, categorize them into three piles, and only keep the things that add value to your life. Start with a tiny area, like a specific drawer or a linen closet, and set a clear timeline to complete the project.

This decluttering process must happen within a specific cadence to maintain food safety and health for food items stored in the pantry and refrigerator. Clean the fridge weekly to remove spoiled foods and wipe down spills to prevent odors. Aim to clear out expired pantry items every few months. Rotate your stock on regularly purchased items to ensure systematic use of the oldest items first. This is also a great way to take inventory and make shopping lists to replenish items, plan to find recipes to use up older items before they expire and ensure you're getting value from all the foods you buy.

Another strategy for clothing closets and dressers is to use the one-year rule. Let it go if you haven't worn an item in the past year. This rule helps to prevent holding onto functional items for sentimental reasons or as an aspirational, goal-weight item. Holding onto clothing that doesn't fit, isn't in style, or is simply outdated only impacts your ability to live in your environment easily. Rotating seasonal items is another way to keep your space more functional. Storage solutions such as baskets, bins, drawer organizers, and shelving units can help to store things in a compact and accessible way to improve ease of use.

This same decluttering process should occur digitally. Regularly cleaning up photos and files from computers, phones, and cloud storage devices, deleting unused apps, and unsubscribing from unnecessary email newsletters frees up space for new experiences.

Be ruthless with paperwork. Sort through bills, receipts, and old paperwork. Shred unnecessary documents and create a filing system for important documents.

Maintaining the Space

To batch tasks and make good use of your free time, it's great to keep a list in your home (mine is on my fridge) for any minor repairs needed in the house. Whenever my list contains three projects, I add any corresponding items that need to be purchased to complete the project onto my shopping list and plan to get that list done over the weekend. These types of projects commonly take up mental bandwidth for months or years simply because there isn't a systematic way of dealing with them. Often, they take very little time and energy to complete, and the sense of accomplishment is great once they are done. It's an excellent opportunity to move the needle and reclaim your space. Take stock of any minor issues throughout your home that have not been prioritized. Walk around with a notepad and reimagine your space as fully optimized. Here is a list of ideas to get you started:

- Patch any small holes in the wall.
- Touch up the paint on walls/trim once you fill small holes.
- Tighten any loose nuts/bolts on furniture.
- Add felt floor protectors to chair legs.

- Change the furnace filter.
- Replace batteries in remotes and fire alarms.
- Dust air returns to the HVAC system.
- Dust the air vents on fridge
- Deep clean the Dryer vent tubing and exit port on the home.
- Replace filters in Air Purifiers/HEPA systems.
- Rewire desk lamps that flicker.
- Remove hair/debris from vacuum cleaners or rolling office chair wheels.
- Explore why the patio, window, or closet doors aren't opening/closing smoothly on their tracks.

Keep a home journal to track improvements and schedule regular maintenance. This "home care" journal helps you organize yourself on regular maintenance and significant capital improvements to the home. Having accurate records that are easily accessible also puts you in the best position to sell the house for top dollar down the road. Simply owning a home journal like this communicates responsible home ownership and care.

Personalize your space

Personalizing your space is a wonderful way to make it feel more comfortable, inviting, and reflective of your personality and interests. Walking into your space should give you an immediate sense of calm and help you feel safe and relaxed.

Displaying personal photos and showcasing your memories in frames that appeal to you is a beautiful way to surround yourself with items that evoke positive emotions. Most drug stores offer photo printing services from your phone, and you can get the items printed while you shop. Digital photos cannot elicit the same visceral body response as printed photographs. Gallery walls mixing pictures, artwork, or mementos are another great way to incorporate a variety of meaningful objects into your day-to-day life.

Express your taste and style through color and texture with pillows, blankets, and decor items throughout your home. These items can easily be changed as you grow and evolve, making them a low-cost way to personalize your space. Reserve big-ticket items such as kitchen tables and couches as more neutral anchor pieces in your home, knowing these will stay the same for a longer period.

Create a sensory calming atmosphere

- Incorporate elements that promote relaxation and tranquility, such as soft lighting, soothing colors, and comfortable furniture.
- Use aromatherapy with essential oils, candles or calming music to create a peaceful ambiance.
- Introduce cozy blankets and pillows with interesting textures within your home.

Bring nature indoors

Introducing natural elements such as indoor plants or natural materials like wood or stone can help connect you to the outdoors and improve air quality. Plants add visual appeal and have been shown to reduce stress, promote health, and boost mood. Several plants are known for their air-purifying qualities, helping to remove common indoor air pollutants such as formaldehyde, benzene, xylene, trichloroethylene, and ammonia. Go to a local nursery and locate the following plants to see which ones most resonate for you visually and select a few to both beautify and purify your space:

1. **Spider Plant (Chlorophytum comosum):** Spider plants are excellent air purifiers and are easy to care for. They help remove formaldehyde, xylene, and toluene from indoor air.

2. **Snake Plant (Sansevieria trifasciata):** Also known as mother-in-law's tongue, snake plants are hardy and require minimal maintenance. They effectively remove benzene, formaldehyde, trichloroethylene, and xylene from the air.

3. **Peace Lily (Spathiphyllum spp.):** Peace lilies are known for their beautiful white flowers and ability to remove formaldehyde, benzene, and trichloroethylene from indoor air. They prefer low-light conditions and regular watering.

4. **Boston Fern (Nephrolepis exaltata):** Boston ferns are lush and attractive plants that help remove formaldehyde, xylene, and toluene from indoor air. They thrive in humid environments with indirect sunlight.

5. **Aloe vera (Aloe barbadensis Miller):** Aloe vera plants have medicinal properties and help remove formaldehyde and benzene from indoor air. Aloe juice or gel extracted from a cut leaf can instantly soothe sunburns or burns received in the kitchen, making them a great addition to a home first aid kit. They prefer bright, indirect sunlight and minimal watering.

6. **Rubber Plant (Ficus elastica):** Rubber plants are hardy

and easy to care for, making them popular indoor plants. They effectively remove formaldehyde from indoor air and prefer bright, indirect light.

7. **Dracaena (Dracaena spp.):** Dracaena varieties such as the Janet Craig, Marginata, and Warneckii are effective air purifiers that can remove multiple indoor air pollutants, including formaldehyde, benzene, trichloroethylene, and xylene.

8. **Bamboo Palm (Chamaedorea seifrizii):** Bamboo palms are tropical plants that thrive in low light conditions and help remove formaldehyde, benzene, and trichloroethylene from indoor air.

9. **English Ivy (Hedera helix)** is a climbing vine that can help reduce airborne mold particles and certain indoor air pollutants, such as formaldehyde. It prefers bright, indirect light and regular watering.

10. **Philodendron (Philodendron spp.):** Philodendrons are popular indoor plants known for their heart-shaped leaves and air-purifying qualities. They effectively remove formaldehyde from indoor air and prefer moderate to bright, indirect light.

Bringing in natural light and aiming to filter/adjust as needed with curtains or blinds is essential. Natural light has been shown to boost mood, enhance productivity, and regulate circadian rhythms. It's as critical to humans as it is for plants.

Create a Sleep-Friendly Space

Sleep is an essential component of physical self-care because it is the foundation of keeping a healthy immune system and reducing stress levels by resetting our nervous system daily.

Good environmental self-care can help support good physical self-care, as many of the self-care categories are connected.

Create a conducive sleep environment by minimizing noise, light, and distractions. Preparing and controlling the space allows you to create successful sleep cycles and genuine rejuvenation. Here are several things to consider:

- Control light exposure. Use blackout curtains, shades, and blinds, or consider an eye mask to eliminate any light in the room. Cover any LED lights on electronic devices in the room with black electrical tape.
- Reduce noise disturbances by using white noise machines, air filters, or fans to promote better sleep quality. Consider using earplugs or other soundproofing techniques to block out unwanted sounds.
- Invest in a high-quality, comfortable mattress, pillow, and bedding that provide adequate support.
- Optimize room temperature. Aim for 60-67 degrees Fahrenheit (15-20 degrees Celsius), as cooler temperatures generally are more conducive to sleep.
- Establish a relaxing bedtime routine to unwind and prepare for sleep. Keep reading materials, candles, or linen sprays handy to create a soothing environment.
- Limit Screen time before bed. Blue light disrupts circadian rhythms and the sleep cycle. It also emits electromagnetic frequencies that disrupt bodily systems. Keep screens out of the bedroom, and don't use them one hour before bedtime.
- Practice good sleep hygiene, using fresh sheets and bed-clothes, avoiding caffeine or heavy meals close to bedtime, and getting regular exercise during the day to ensure a

healthy, regulated internal clock.

Create Safe, Functional Zones in the Home

Organize your space into functional zones for different activities, such as a designated work area, relaxation corner, or exercise space. Clear delineation of spaces helps create a sense of purpose and order. Use bookshelves, room dividers, or furniture to define those spaces if necessary. Then, work to ensure that each space is safe and effective for that specific end-use. This is also helpful in creating hidden "drop zones" to contain clutter quickly when necessary for unexpected guests or to stage items for further organization for future donations or sales.

- Ensure your environment is safe, accessible, and conducive to your needs and abilities. Consider traffic flow, minimize obstacles, and provide easy solutions for family members to store items safely when they enter the home.
- Implement ergonomic solutions: Arrange furniture and equipment in a way that promotes good posture and reduces physical strain. Invest in ergonomic chairs, standing desks, or adjustable monitor stands to support comfort and productivity.
- Remove hazards from high-traffic areas.
- Install safety gates or barriers to block off stairs or hazardous areas from young children or pets.
- Secure heavy furniture to walls to prevent tip-overs.
- Use outlet covers and cord organizers to minimize electrical hazards.
- Install handrails or grab bars in tubs, showers, or stairs if needed.

- Make adjustments to accommodate any mobility or accessibility requirements.

Create a technology-free zone.

- Designate specific areas of your space as technology-free zones to promote digital detoxing and unplugging from screens.
- Establish boundaries around technology use and when audible notifications are allowed to create opportunities for rest, relaxation, and face-to-face interaction without digital distractions.
- Consider a "no phones" rule at the kitchen table to promote better connection and communication.

Limit exposure to environmental Toxins.

- Identify and minimize exposure to environmental stressors such as pollutants, allergens, or excessive noise.
- Use air purifiers, noise-canceling headphones, or sound-proofing materials to create a healthier and more comfortable environment.
- Commit to purchasing fragrance-free body care and cleaning supplies.
- Protect your sleep space from radio frequencies. Keep cell phones out of the bedroom.
- Consider dropping all shoes at the front door or leaving them on the porch.
- Use only low-VOC paint and building materials in the home.
- Filter tap water. Choose a filter to remove impurities such

as chlorine, lead, and pesticides, or install a reverse osmosis machine.

- Opt for Eco-friendly or non-toxic cleaning products free of harsh chemicals. You can also save money by making your cleaners and double up on the benefits.
- Use a HEPA filter to control your home's dust, allergens, and toxins. Dust surfaces regularly with a damp cloth to prevent particles from being reintroduced into the air.
- Test for radon, lead, mold, and asbestos and take proper measures to address any identified issues.

Environmental self-care is more than cleaning and organizing—it's about curating a space that aligns with your values, supports your well-being, and allows you to thrive. By decluttering, personalizing, and optimizing your environment, you can create a sanctuary that nurtures relaxation, focus, and renewal. Your space is not just where you live—it's a reflection of how you care for yourself.

Journal Prompts for Environmental Health and Well-Being

1. How does my living space currently make me feel, and what changes would enhance my comfort and well-being?
2. What are three small decluttering projects I can start with to bring a sense of order to my home?
3. Which room or area in my home do I find the most relaxing, and what makes it feel that way?
4. How do I balance functionality and aesthetics in my living space, and is there room for improvement?
5. What items in my home hold sentimental value, and how

can I display or store them meaningfully?

6. How do I currently manage clutter, and are there systems I could implement to improve organization?

7. What steps can I take to incorporate more natural elements, like plants or sunlight, into my living space?

8. What role does lighting, scents, or sounds play in creating a calming atmosphere in my home?

9. Are there any areas in my home that feel stagnant or neglected, and how can I refresh them?

10. What toxic products or materials could I replace with eco-friendly or non-toxic alternatives in my home?

11. How does my bedroom support my sleep, and what adjustments could make it more restful and rejuvenating?

12. What does my ideal sanctuary look like, and how can I recreate elements of it in my current living space?

13. How do I feel about my digital spaces, such as my computer and phone, and what steps can I take to declutter them?

14. What habits can I develop to maintain a consistently clean and organized environment?

15. What are some creative or budget-friendly ways to personalize my space and make it uniquely mine?

16. How do I use my outdoor space or connect with nature, and how can I enhance this connection?

17. What functional zones in my home support my daily routines, and how can I optimize them?

18. How can I create technology-free zones in my home to encourage relaxation and face-to-face connection?

19. What small maintenance tasks or home projects have I been putting off, and how can I prioritize them?

20. What steps can I take to reduce environmental toxins in

my home, such as improving air quality or switching to natural cleaners?

13

THE ROAD TO CHANGE

Self-care is not a fleeting trend or a buzzword but an essential part of our human experience. It often operates unconsciously as we navigate life's stressors, but by bringing it into conscious awareness, we can find a more intentional path to peace, balance, and fulfillment.

This journey has explored the multifaceted nature of self-care, emphasizing that it looks different for everyone. By using self-assessment tools, we've identified areas where we can better support ourselves and reprioritize our energy to create space for what truly matters. Along the way, we've delved into a toolbox of ideas and strategies to inspire your personalized self-care plan.

The principles of mindfulness, boundaries, gratitude, and intentional, assertive communication are at the heart of every self-care practice. These principles guide us in fostering healthier relationships with ourselves, others, and our environment. Whether we learn to say "no" without guilt, cultivate nourishing self-talk, or manage emotional triggers, these foundational skills enable us to move through life with greater ease and resilience.

We've also examined the critical role of nervous system regulation. A system stuck in a heightened stress response cannot sustain long-term self-care efforts. Shifting into a calm, parasympathetic state creates the optimal foundation for building and maintaining meaningful self-care practices.

This journey has shown us the importance of saying "yes" to nourishing our bodies with nutritious foods, prioritizing restorative sleep, and engaging in physical activity to sustain vitality. On the emotional and social fronts, we've embraced emotional regulation, cultivated meaningful relationships, and learned to foster intimacy and connection. Professionally and financially, we've explored work-life balance, realistic goal-setting, and the significance of financial wellness in creating stability and abundance.

Beyond the physical and emotional, we've uncovered the spiritual dimension of self-care, finding purpose and meaning through mindfulness, gratitude, and connection with nature. We've rejected the pressures of hustle culture and perfectionism, recognizing the necessity of slowing down and nurturing our inner world.

Self-care is not selfish—it is essential. It's about sustaining your energy reserves so you can show up fully for yourself and others. When we nurture our well-being, we model healthy behaviors for those around us, inviting them to prioritize their own care.

Incorporating self-care into daily life may initially feel daunting, especially when time constraints, guilt, or self-doubt arise. But meaningful change begins with small, intentional steps. Each choice you make to care for yourself is a vote for the life you want to create.

When life becomes overwhelming, visualize a future where self-care is non-negotiable—a steady foundation that supports your vitality and fulfillment. Imagine waking up energized and aligned with your values, ready to embrace each day with clarity and purpose. See yourself thriving, living a life of joy and balance, and sharing that abundance with the world.

As you embark on this journey of self-discovery, trust your intuition. Follow the paths that spark curiosity, joy, or a sense of breakthrough. Each small step forward is a triumph; every moment of care you give yourself builds the foundation for a more balanced, fulfilling life. Celebrate your progress—no matter how small—and know that meaningful change unfolds in its own time.

When challenges arise—and they will—remember that faltering is a natural part of growth. Think of it not as a setback but as an opportunity to practice resilience and recommit to your well-being. Each time you return to your self-care practices, you reinforce your dedication to yourself and your journey. The beauty of self-care lies in its flexibility; it is always there for you, waiting to support and nurture you.

The road to change begins with you. You've got this.

14

A NOTE OF GRATITUDE

As we draw the final pages of "The Ultimate Self-Care Handbook: 1000+ Hassle-Free Ideas to Escape Burnout, Reduce Stress and Reclaim Your Life" to a close, I want to take a moment to express my heartfelt gratitude to you, the reader. Your commitment to embark on this journey of self-care and personal transformation is a brave act of self-love and a decisive step towards a more fulfilled and balanced life.

Thank you for allowing me to be a part of your self-care journey. Whether you've dipped into a self-care assessment quiz to increase awareness, sought out ideas to flesh out your existing self-care toolkit, or methodically worked through each suggestion to identify areas for further research and exploration to build a sustainable, personalized self-care regimen, your willingness to engage with this material and integrate it into your life is deeply appreciated.

Your stories, which some of you have shared, inspire and motivate me to continue exploring new paths to wellness and happiness. Each step to nurture your well-being helps light the way for others, creating positive change.

I am grateful for the opportunity to connect with so many beautiful souls committed to caring for themselves with the same passion and dedication they care for others. Your journey reinforces the importance of self-care and the powerful impact it has not only on our lives but on the world.

As you continue to use this handbook, remember that each act of self-care, no matter how small, is a profound affirmation of your worth and a step towards a vibrant, fulfilling life. Thank you for your trust, time, and commitment to your health and happiness. May you always find peace and strength in the practices you've discovered here, and may your path be filled with light and joy.

With deepest gratitude and warmest wishes,

Lorilee

Now that you have everything you need to reduce stress, escape burnout, and reclaim your life, it's time to pass on your newfound knowledge and show other readers where they can find the same help.

By leaving your honest opinion of this book on Amazon, you'll show other people just like you where they can find the information they're looking for to achieve their own health and wellness goals.

Changing the cultural norm to ensure everyone knows that self-care is their basic right can only catch on when we pass on our knowledge, and you're helping to do just that.

Scan the QR code above to review the paperback or click here to review the e-book.

Thank you for being a part of this journey and for helping others find their way to wellness. Your review can make a big difference.

"What we do for ourselves dies with us. What we do for others and the world remains and is immortal." — Albert Pine

15

RESOURCES

12 months of self care: the plan. (2018, June 4). Over the Deep End. https://www.overthedeepend.com/being-enough/12-months-of-self-care-the-plan/

Developing your Self-Care Plan. (2019, October 28). University at Buffalo School of Social Work - University at Buffalo. https://socialwork.buffalo.edu/resources/self-care-starter-kit/developing-your-self-care-plan.html

Girlboss, & Girlboss. (2021, November 1). *Knowing your "Money Story" (And how to Begin Re-Writing it).* Girlboss. https://girlboss.com/blogs/read/whats-a-money-story

Sweetwaterhrv. (2012, February 2). *The parasympathetic side of your nervous system.* SweetWater Health. https://sweetwaterhrv.com/blog/balance-your-nervous-system/the-parasympathetic-side-of-your-nervous-system/

Otero, I. (2023, June 8). *The Art of Grounding/Earthing &*

Its Benefits. CYMBIOTIKA. https://cymbiotika.com/blogs/news/the-art-of-grounding-earthing-its-benefits?utm_source=google&utm_medium=cpc&utm_campaign=21102941006&utm_term=&nbt=nb%3Aadwords%3Ax%3A21102941006%3A%3A&nb_adtype=&nb_kwd=&nb_ti=&nb_mi=&nb_pc=&nb_pi=&nb_ppi=&nb_placement=&nb_li_ms=&nb_lp_ms=&nb_fii=&nb_ap=&nb_mt=&gad_source=1&gclid=CjwKCAjwt-OwBhBnEiwAgwzrUtrQkbXGM-ZK36y6OEQx6b-y4TOhgc_a20W39mD9AXnTcIDriyHLVBoC4dEQAvD_BwE

Oschman, J. L., Chevalier, G., & Brown, R. L. (2015). The effects of grounding (earthing) on inflammation, the immune response, wound healing, and prevention and treatment of chronic inflammatory and autoimmune diseases. *Journal of Inflammation Research*, 83. https://doi.org/10.2147/jir.s69656

Take care of your body, mind and spiritual health | Banner. (n.d.). https://www.bannerhealth.com/healthcareblog/better-me/8-ways-to-take-care-of-your-spiritual-health

Christian, K. (2023, December 21). *5 Ideas for creating a Spiritual Practice—Whether you're religious or not - The good trade.* The Good Trade. https://www.thegoodtrade.com/features/cultivating-spirituality/

Delaney, C. (2023, July 25). *How to be happy and have more fun – differently.* EcoFriendlyLink - Naturally Healthy Green Living. https://ecofriendlylink.com/blog/be-happy-have-more-fun/

Rucker, M. (2023, September 15). *How to start having more fun*. Psyche. https://psyche.co/guides/how-to-start-having-more-fun-in-your-busy-life

Aid, T. (2018, July 10). *Self-Care Assessment*. Therapist Aid. https://www.therapistaid.com/therapy-worksheet/self-care-assessment

Self-Care assessments, exercises and activities. (2018, December 4). University at Buffalo School of Social Work - University at Buffalo. https://socialwork.buffalo.edu/resources/self-care-starter-kit/self-care-assessments-exercises.html

Van Der Sande, E. (2021, March 23). *Self-Care and the parasympathetic nervous system*. Trauma Sensitive Yoga – the Netherlands. https://www.traumasensitiveyoganederland.com/self-care-and-the-parasympathetic-nervous-system/

Adriana. (2021, March 10). *10 Types of Self-Care & How to Practice Them - Adriana Thani*. Adriana Thani. https://adrianathani.com/types-of-self-care/

Gibson, C. (2023, September 14). *The 8 Types of Self Care And Why They're All Important*. Creating Self Love. https://creatingselflove.com/the-8-types-of-self-care/#what-is-self-care

Thalia. (2023, December 29). *51 Environmental Self-Care Ideas to Help Boost your Physical and Mental Well-Being*. Notes by Thalia. https://notesbythalia.com/environmental-self-care-ideas/

Emotional Regulation: Skills, Exercises, & Strategies to Regulate.
(n.d.). https://www.betterup.com/blog/emotional-regulatio
n-skills

Surprising remote work burnout statistics in 2024. (n.d.). https://w
ww.travelperk.com/blog/remote-work-burnout-statistics/

Hinde K, White G, Armstrong N. Wearable Devices Suit-
able for Monitoring Twenty Four Hour Heart Rate Variability in Military Populations. Sensors (Basel). 2021 Feb
4;21(4):1061. doi: 10.3390/s21041061. PMID: 33557190;
PMCID: PMC7913967.

Surprising remote work burnout statistics in 2024. (n.d.-b).
https://www.travelperk.com/blog/remote-work-burnout-s
tatistics/

Yeh, E. (2020, October 13). Emotional Guidance scale. *Oriental
Art Supply.* https://orientalartsupply.com/blogs/news/emoti
onal-guidance-scale

victoriaGB. (2023, October 11). *how to use the abraham-hicks
emotional guidance scale.* gabbybernstein.com. https://gabbybe
rnstein.com/emotional-guidance-scale-abraham-hicks/

Routley, N. (2021, April 9). *A visual guide to human emotion.*
Visual Capitalist. https://www.visualcapitalist.com/a-visual-
guide-to-human-emotion/

Financial Tips: Six steps to creating a Positive money mindset.
(2022, June 1). Happy State Bank. https://www.happybank.c

om/resources/six-steps-to-creating-a-positive-money-mind set

PsyD, B. W. (n.d.). *The Five Levels of Intimacy | FamilyLife Canada*. https://www.familylifecanada.com/blog/the-five-levels-of-i ntimacy/

Hayes, A. (2023, November 29). *Average raise percentage: What factors affect your raise?* Investopedia. https://www.investo pedia.com/articles/personal-finance/090415/salary-secrets-what-considered-big-raise.asp

Loneliness and social isolation linked to serious health conditions. (n.d.-b). https://www.cdc.gov/aging/publications/features/lonely-older-adults.html

Shetty, M. (2023, December 18). *How social connection supports longevity | Social Engagement*. Lifestyle Medicine. https://longe vity.stanford.edu/lifestyle/2023/12/18/how-social-connecti on-supports-longevity/

Wong, K. (2020, August 17). *How to Add More Play to Your Grown-Up Life, Even Now*. The New York Times. https://www. nytimes.com/2020/08/14/smarter-living/adults-play-work-life-balance.html

Williams, R. (2019, March 28). *10 Spiritual Self-Care Tips to be Happy*. Chopra. https://chopra.com/blogs/personal-growth/10-spiritual-self-care-tips-to-be-happy

Ludwig, S. (2021, August 14). Create your own spiritual rituals.

Canyon Ranch. https://www.canyonranch.com/well-stated/post/create-your-own-spiritual-rituals/

Capp, K. M. B. (2024, March 13). *Science of Spirituality (+16 Ways to Become More Spiritual).* PositivePsychology.com. https://positivepsychology.com/science-of-spirituality/#practice

Hope grows | Caregiver Support – Providing care for the caregiver. (n.d.). https://hopegrows.org/news/what-is-spiritual-purpose/

Writing@CSU. (n.d.). https://writing.colostate.edu/guides/teaching/co300man/pop12d.cfm

Wright, J., & Wright, J. (2023, March 10). *Small ways to make a big difference in your community.* Sleep in Heavenly Peace. https://shpbeds.org/blog/making-a-difference-in-your-community/

Birt, J. (2023, August 23). *14 Ways To Practice Self-Care at Work (And Why It Matters).* indeed.com. Retrieved April 16, 2024, from https://www.indeed.com/career-advice/career-development/selfcare-at-work

Diana Pressey. (2024, January 9). *50 Self-Care & Workplace Wellness Ideas for You, Your Team & Your Company.* InHerSight. https://www.inhersight.com/blog/insight-commentary/self-care-and-workplace-wellness-ideas

Psychology Tools. (2023, November 30). *Psychological Assess-*

ment Scales and Measures | Psychology Tools. https://www.psyc
hologytools.com/download-scales-and-measures/

Justin. (2024, April 16). *Take a mental health test.* Mental Health
America. https://screening.mhanational.org/screening-tools
/

Boldt, L. J., Kochanska, G., & Jonas, K. (2016). Infant attachment moderates paths from early negativity to preadolescent
outcomes for children and parents. *Child Development, 88*(2),
584–596. https://doi.org/10.1111/cdev.12607

Bartholomew, K., & Horowitz, L. M. (1991). Attachment styles
among young adults: A test of a four-category model. *Journal
of Personality and Social Psychology, 61*(2), 226–244. https://doi.
org/10.1037/0022-3514.61.2.226

Ginsberg, E., & Ginsberg, E. (2023, September 27). 7 Fall Girls'
Day ideas so fun they'll make it out of the group chat. *The
Everygirl.* https://theeverygirl.com/fall-girls-day-ideas/

Vickie, & Vickie. (2023b, July 7). Abraham Hicks Emotional
Guidance Scale – Comprehensive Guide. *Discovering Peace.*
https://www.discoveringpeace.com/the-abraham-hicks-em
otional-guidance-scale.html

16

About the Author

Lorilee Lucas, a California native, offers a unique blend of scientific insight, holistic wellness, and creative approaches to energetic healing work. With academic and professional backgrounds in Biological Sciences, Massage Therapy, Yoga and Fashion Design, Lorilee's unique expertise straddles the scientific, healing, and creative realms.

Informed by personal loss, professional pivots, and an unshakeable belief in the transformative power of inner knowing, Lorilee encourages others to explore their own internal wisdom while finding support and drawing inspiration from the years of research that inform the resources provided in the book.

Her profound connection to self-care became all the more personal following a life-altering near-death experience in 2007, which thrust her into a relentless pursuit to reclaim her life. Many of the self-care techniques in this book were explored on the long road to recovery while detoxifying her system, rebuilding muscle strength, and restoring her zest for life.

Her commitment to self-care deepened significantly in 2020 after a cascade of losses, including navigating the aftermath of losing her home in a California wildfire, loss of financial stability to COVID-19, and dissolution of her long-term marriage. During this period, she was also diagnosed with systemic mold illness, affecting multiple organ systems. Balanced self-care became crucial to her recovery process. With so many of the self-care categories being simultaneously affected, her ability to self-assess allowed her to strategically adapt to focus on the most impactful areas for positive change, allowing her to navigate these losses with resilience.

"The Ultimate Self-Care Handbook: 1000+ Hassle-Free Ideas to Escape Burnout, Reduce Stress, and Reclaim Your Life" is based on extensive research and lived experience. Starting with a comprehensive self-assessment quiz, readers can gauge their initial state of well-being. This foundational insight allows them to effectively navigate the toolbox of resources and tailor an individualized self-care strategy that resonates with their unique lifestyle and enhances their overall quality of life.

Beyond the pages of her books, Lorilee thrives in the vibrant world of fashion design, teaches yoga, invests in real estate as both a landlord and private money lender, and leads several women-focused investment groups. Her passion for an adventurous road trip and enjoying the great outdoors mirrors her approach to life: a continuous exploration of the world's beauty and possibility. She finds immeasurable joy in uplifting others and helping them uncover meaning, passion, and purpose. She invites you to join her in discovering the simple pleasures and profound lessons that each day offers through radical acts of self-care.

www.ingramcontent.com/pod-product-compliance
Lightning Source LLC
Chambersburg PA
CBHW061752120626
46550CB00005B/1967